PIANO • VOCAL • GUITAR

93 SONGS FROM YOUR FAVORITE SHOWS

ISBN 0-634-04382-X

7777 W. BLUEMOUND RD. P.O. BOX 13819 MILWAUKEE, WI 53213

Visit Hal Leonard Online at
www.halleonard.com

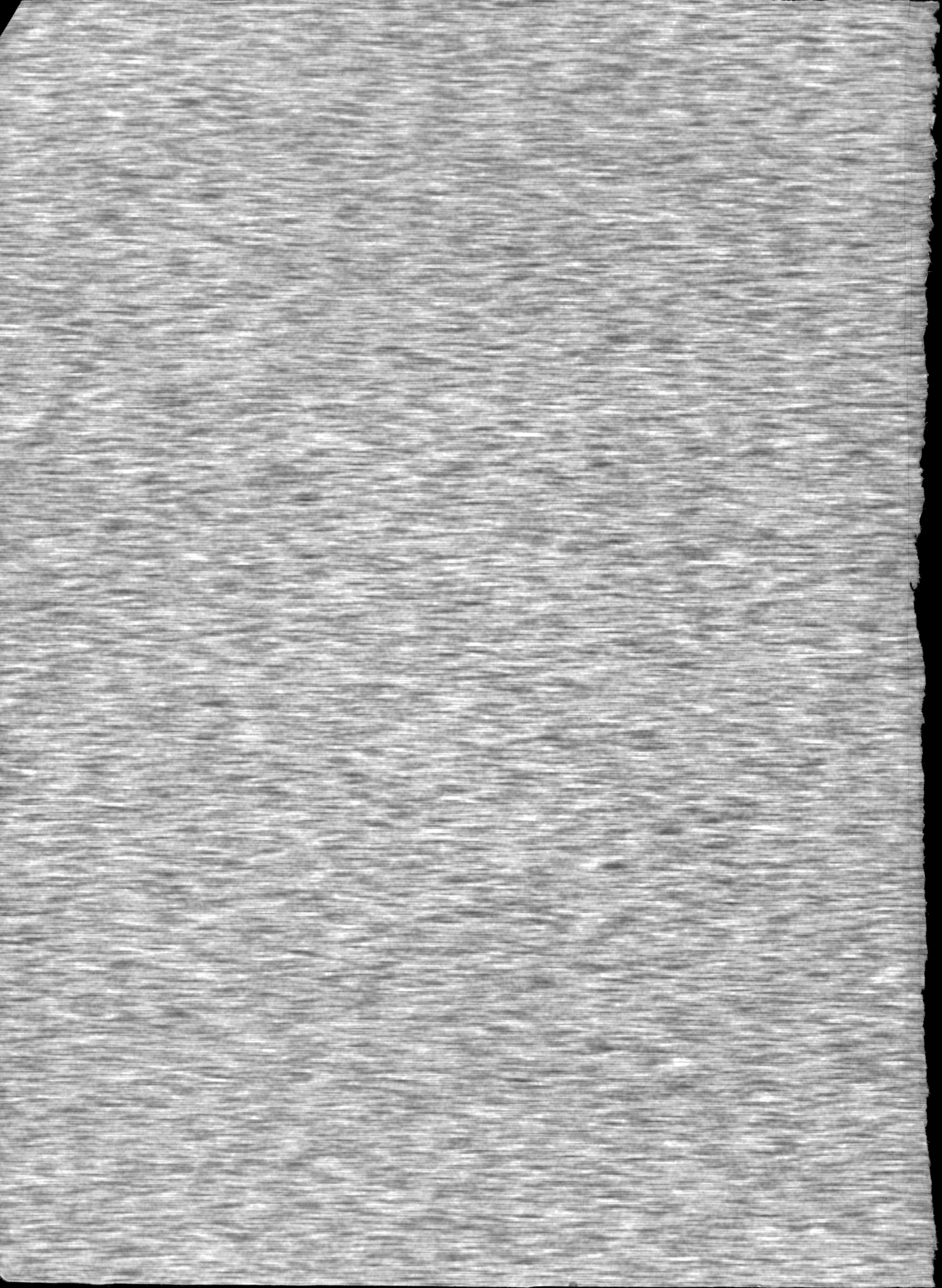

PIANO • VOCAL • GUITAR
ULTIMATE

TV THEMES

93 SONGS FROM YOUR FAVORITE SHOWS

THEME FROM "THE A TEAM"
from the Television Series

By MIKE POST
and PETE CARPENTER

F
Gm
3fr
F/A
Cm/B♭
B♭
Cm/B♭
B♭
B♭/C
F
D5
C5
D5
C5
D5
C5
G
F
D5
C5
B♭5
C5
D5
C5
D5
C5
D5
C5
G
F
D5
C5
D5
C5
B♭5
A5

Db/Eb
Eb/Bb
3fr
Db/Eb
Fm7
Gbmaj9
Fm7/Bb
Gm7/C
Abm7/Db
4fr
Db/Ab
Cb/Db
4fr
Gbsus
7
F
Bb
C
F
Eb
3fr
Bb/D
C
F
Gm
3fr
F/A
Bb
F/Bb
Bb
F/Bb
Gm
3fr
F/A
F/Bb
C
F

ALFRED HITCHCOCK PRESENTS

Theme from the Television Series

By D. KAHN and M. LENARD
based on a theme of CHARLES GOUNOD

THE ADDAMS FAMILY THEME

Theme from the TV Show and Movie

Music and Lyrics by
VIC MIZZY

F7
B♭
Cm7
3fr
F7
B♭
N.C.
peo - ple come to see 'em, they real - ly are a scree - um, the Ad - dams Fam - i - ly.
(Spoken:) Neat.
Sweet.
B♭
Cm7
3fr
F7
B♭
Petite. (Sung:) So get a witch - 's shawl on, a broom - stick you can crawl on, we're
Cm7
3fr
F7
B♭
gon - na pay a call on the Ad - dams Fam - i - ly.

THE BALLAD OF DAVY CROCKETT

from Walt Disney's DAVY CROCKETT

Words by TOM BLACKBURN
Music by GEORGE BRUNS

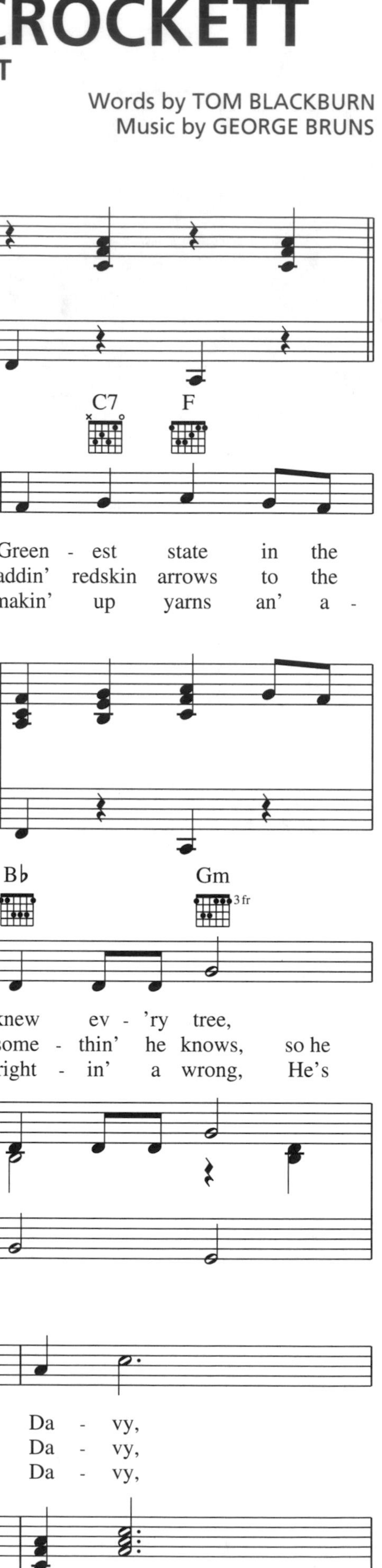

1-9
10
B♭
F
C7
F
F
Da - vy Crock-ett, King of the wild fron - tier! 2. In fear!
Da - vy Crock-ett, man who _ don't know fear!
Da - vy Crock-ett, buck - skin _ buc - ca - neer!
F
C7
F
B♭
F
C7
F
G7
C7
11.-17. (See additional lyrics)
18. he come home his pol - i - tick-in' done, The west - ern march had just be - gun, So he
19. heard of Houston an' Au - stin an' so, To the Texas plains he jest had to go, Where
20. land is biggest an' his land is best, From grass - y plains to the moun - tain _ crest, He's a -
F
F/A
B♭
Gm
3fr
C7
F
packed his gear an' his trust - y gun, An' lit out grin-nin' to fol - low the sun.
Free - dom was fight - in' an - oth - er foe, An' they needed him at the A - la - mo.
head of us all meetin' the test, Follow - in' his leg - end in - to the West.
11-19
20
B♭
F
C7
F
F
clear! 18. When
Da - vy, Da - vy Crock - ett, lead - in' the pi - o - neer! 19. He
Da - vy, Da - vy Crock - ett, the man who _ don't know fear! 20. His
Da - vy, Da - vy Crock - ett, King of the wild fron - tier!

Additional Lyrics

4. Andy Jackson is our gen'ral's name,
His reg'lar soldiers we'll put to shame,
Them redskin varmints us Volunteers'll tame,
'Cause we got the guns with the sure-fire aim.
Davy - Davy Crockett,
The champion of us all!

5. Headed back to war from the ol' home place,
But Red Stick was leadin' a merry chase,
Fightin' an' burnin' at a devil's pace
South to the swamps on the Florida Trace.
Davy - Davy Crockett,
Trackin' the redskins down!

6. Fought single-handed through the Injun War
Till the Creeks was whipped an' peace was in store,
An' while he was handlin' this risky chore,
Made hisself a legend for evermore.
Davy - Davy Crockett,
King of the wild frontier!

7. He give his word an' he give his hand
That his Injun friends could keep their land,
An' the rest of his life he took the stand
That justice was due every redskin band.
Davy - Davy Crockett,
Holdin' his promise dear!

8. Home fer the winter with his family,
Happy as squirrels in the ol' gum tree,
Bein' the father he wanted to be,
Close to his boys as the pod an' the pea.
Davy - Davy Crockett,
Holdin' his young 'uns dear!

9. But the ice went out an' the warm winds came
An' the meltin' snow showed tracks of game,
An' the flowers of Spring filled the woods with flame,
An' all of a sudden life got too tame.
Davy - Davy Crockett,
Headin' on West again!

10. Off through the woods we're ridin' along,
Makin' up yarns an' singin' a song,
He's ringy as a b'ar an twice as strong,
An' knows he's right 'cause he ain't often wrong.
Davy - Davy Crockett,
The man who don't know fear!

11. Lookin' fer a place where the air smells clean,
Where the tree is tall an' the grass is green,
Where the fish is fat in an untouched stream,
An' the teemin' woods is a hunter's dream.
Davy - Davy Crockett,
Lookin' fer Paradise!

12. Now he'd lost his love an' his grief was gall,
In his heart he wanted to leave it all,
An' lose himself in the forests tall,
But he answered instead his country's call.
Davy - Davy Crockett,
Beginnin' his campaign!

13. Needin' his help they didn't vote blind,
They put in Davy 'cause he was their kind,
Sent up to Nashville the best they could find,
A fightin' spirit an' a thinkin' mind.
Davy - Davy Crockett,
Choice of the whole frontier!

14. The votes were counted an' he won hands down,
So they sent him off to Washin'ton town
With his best dress suit still his buckskins brown,
A livin' legend of growin' renown.
Davy - Davy Crockett,
The Canebrake Congressman!

15. He went off to Congress an' served a spell,
Fixin' up the Gover'ment an' laws as well,
Took over Washin'ton so we heered tell
An' patched up the crack in the Liberty Bell.
Davy - Davy Crockett,
Seein' his duty clear!

16. Him an' his jokes travelled all through the land,
An' his speeches made him friends to beat the band,
His politickin' was their favorite brand
An' everyone wanted to shake his hand.
Davy - Davy Crockett,
Helpin' his legend grow!

17. He knew when he spoke he sounded the knell
Of his hopes for White House an' fame as well,
But he spoke out strong so hist'ry books tell
An patched up the crack in the Liberty Bell.
Davy - Davy Crockett,
Seein' his duty clear!

BANDSTAND BOOGIE

from the Television Series AMERICAN BANDSTAND

Special Lyric by BARRY MANILOW
and BRUCE SUSSMAN
Music by CHARLES ALBERTINE

D/E
B7
B♭maj7
1.
A
2.
A
A
A/C♯
D
E♭dim7
A/E
B7/D♯
A
D9
C♯7♯5
C13
B7
B♭maj7
A
G♯
A
A/C♯
D
E♭dim7

A/E
B7/D♯
A
D9
C♯7♯5
C13
To Coda
B7
B♭maj7
A
A6
D9
D/E
B7
B♭maj7
A

Bm/A
B/A
Adim7
3
3
3
3
Bm7/E
A6
D9
C#7#5
C13
B7
B♭maj7
A

A6
D9
B7
B♭maj7
A
D.S. al Coda
CODA
A
3
A6
Dm6/B
A6

B♭6
E♭9

E♭/F

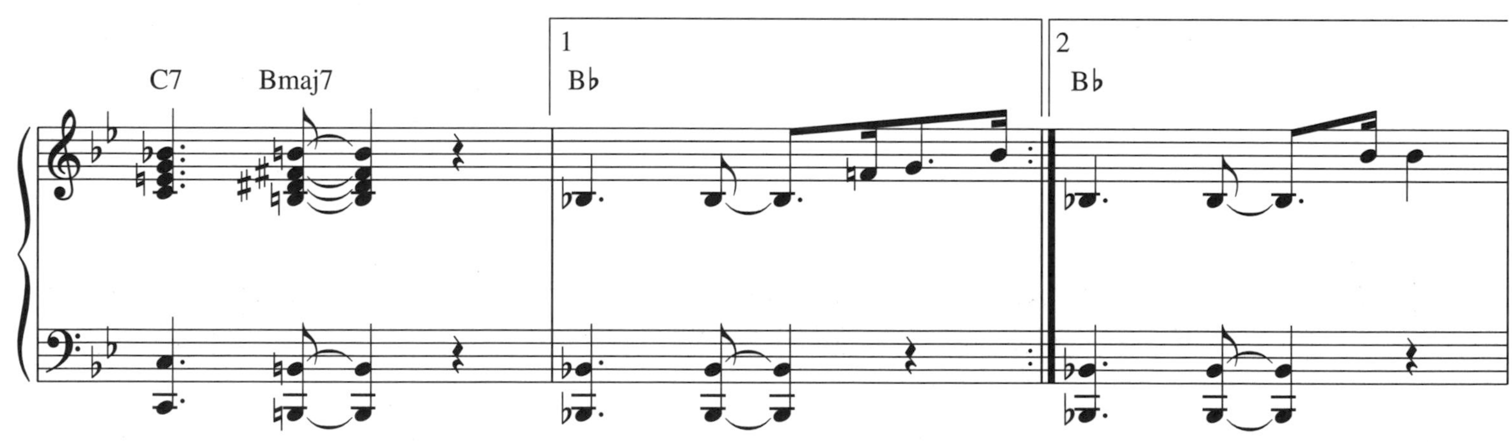
C7
Bmaj7
1
B♭
2
B♭

N.C.

E♭9
D7♯5
D♭13
C7
Bmaj7

B♭6

E♭9
E♭/F

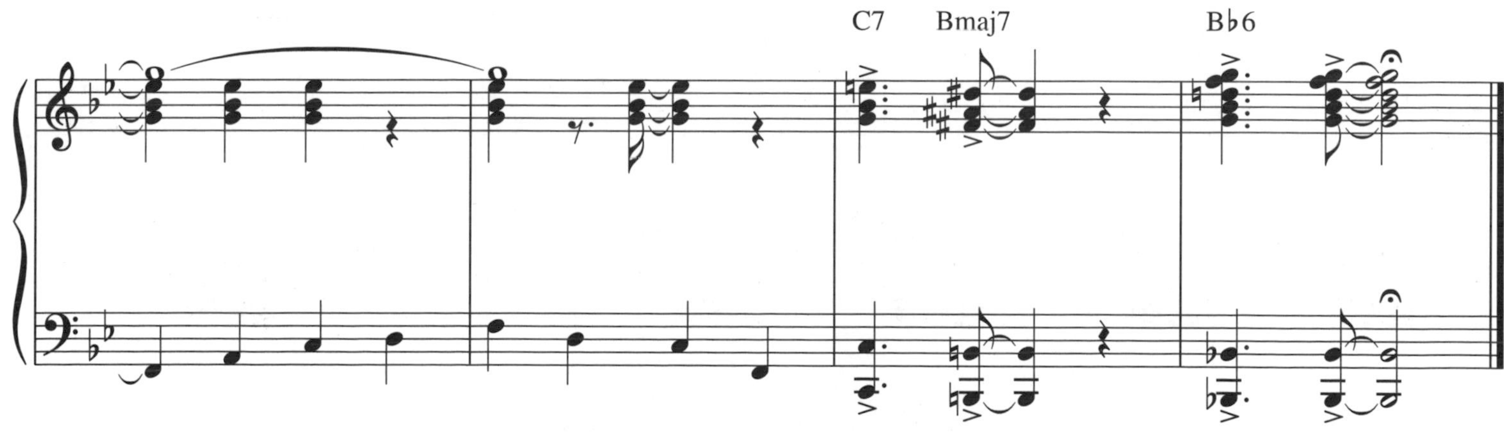
C7
Bmaj7
B♭6

THEME FROM "BEAUTY AND THE BEAST"
from the Television Series

Music by
LEE ELWOOD HOLDRIDGE

Am
Em
F(add 9)
G
Am
Em
F(add 9)
G
A
G
dim.
Fmaj7
Bm7♭5
E7
Asus(add 2)
F♯dim7
C/G
Csus/G
C/G
mp
Fm6/A♭
C
Fm7
B♭
cresc.

E♭
Fm/A♭
E♭
Fm/A♭
A♭5
E♭
A♭5
f
E♭
B♭7/A♭
B♭7/D
Cm
3fr
Gm
3fr
A♭(add9)
B♭
Cm
3fr
Gm
3fr
A♭(add9)
B♭
E♭
F/E♭
dim.
mp
B♭
F/E♭
E♭
rit.

BEIN' GREEN

Words and Music by
JOE RAPOSO

Cm7
nic - er be - in' red, or yel - low, or
F9
gold, or some - thing much more col - or - ful like
B♭
6fr.
A♭
4fr.
G♭
F7
that. It's not
B♭maj7
6fr.
B♭6
5fr.
B♭
6fr.
A7+5
5fr.
eas - y be - in' green, it seems you blend in with so man - y oth - er

Fm6
G11
G7-9
or - di - nar - y things,
and peo - ple tend to pass you
Cm7
o - ver,
'cause you're not stand - ing out
like flash - y
F9
spar - kles on the wa - ter
or stars in the
B♭
6fr.
sky.
But green is the
cresc.

Ab maj7
Db maj7
col - or of spring,
and green can be cool and
Bb
6fr.
friend - ly like,
And green can be
Gm7
Gm(maj7)
Gm7
C9
big like an o - cean or im - por - tant like a moun - tain or
cresc.
f
Cm7
F7
tall like a tree.
When green is
p

B♭maj7
6fr.
B♭6
5fr.
B♭
6fr.
A7+5
5fr.
all there is to be, it could make you
Fm6
G11
G7
won - der why, but why won - der, why won - der? I am
Cm7
F9
green and it - 'll do fine, it's beau - ti - ful and I think it's
dim.
B♭
6fr.
what I want to be.
pp

THEME FROM "BEN CASEY"

from BEN CASEY

By DAVID RAKSIN

With drive (♩ = 120)

To Coda
1
2
(Optional in R.H.)
mf
3

D.S. al Coda
f
sfz
sfz
CODA
ff
fff

BEVERLY HILLS 90210
(Main Theme)
from the Television Series BEVERLY HILLS 90210

By JOHN E. DAVIS

2
B♭
D♭5
4 fr
A♭5
4 fr

B♭

D♭5
4 fr
E♭5
F(add2)

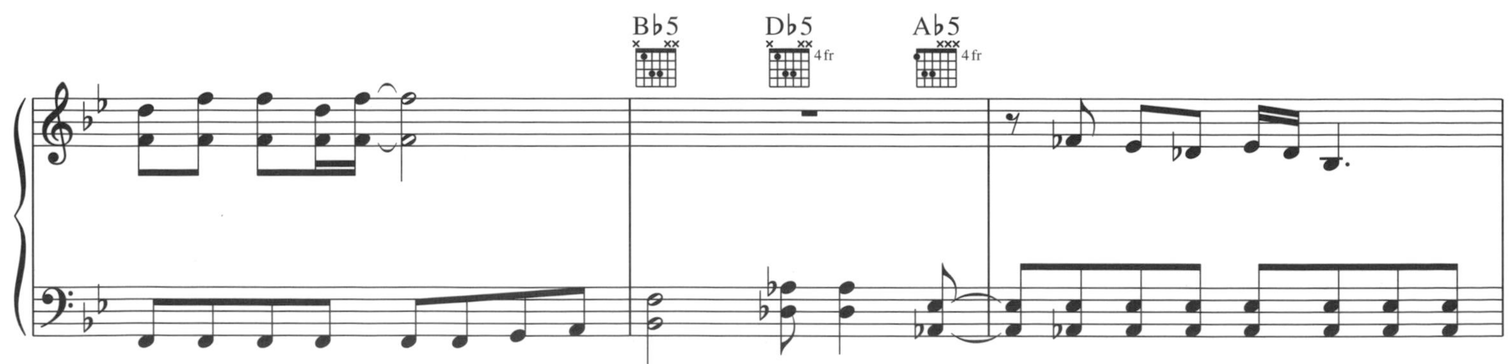
B♭5
D♭5
4 fr
A♭5
4 fr

Bb5
Db5
4 fr
Eb5
Bb5
Db5
4 fr
Ab5
4 fr

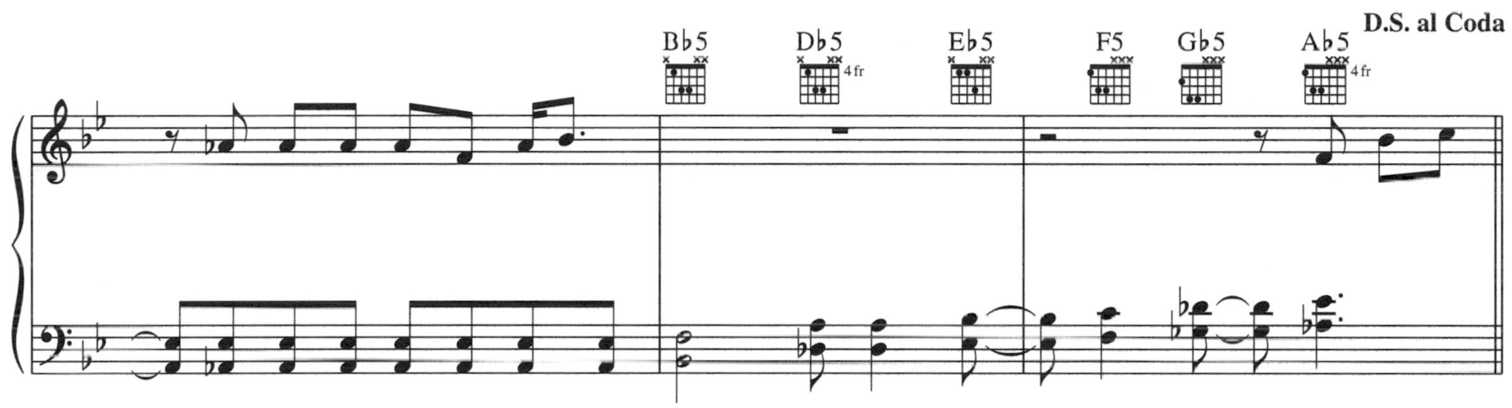
Bb5
Db5
4 fr
Eb5
F5
Gb5
Ab5
4 fr
D.S. al Coda

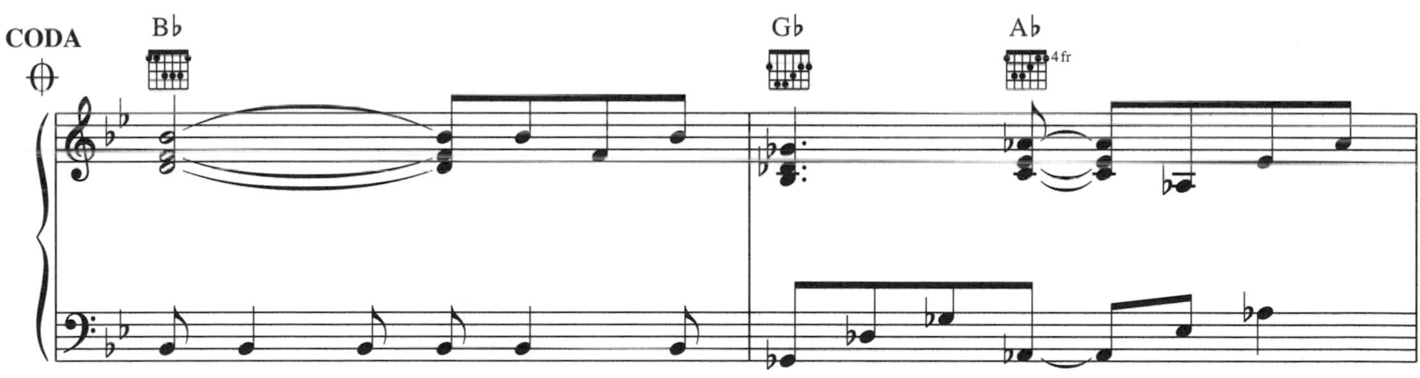
CODA
Bb
Gb
Ab
4 fr

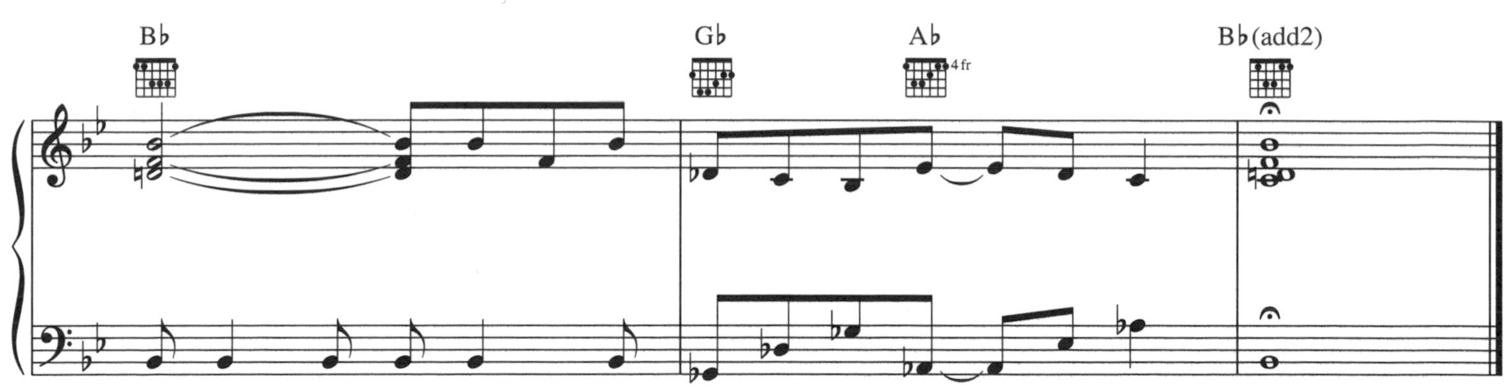
Bb
Gb
Ab
4 fr
Bb(add2)

THEME FROM "BEWITCHED"

from the Television Series

Words and Music by JACK KELLER
and HOWARD GREENFIELD

Fm6
Em7
E7♭9
Am
you were do - ing, I looked in your eyes. That
Am7
D9
4fr
G7sus
brand of woo that you've been brew - in' took me by sur - prise.
G7
C♯dim7
Dm7
G7
You witch, you witch,
Dm7
G7
E♭dim7
Em7
one thing is for sure that stuff you pitch

A7
Em7
just has - n't got a cure.
A7
Fmaj7
My heart was un - der
F♯dim7
C/G
B♭
A7
lock and key but some - how it got un - hitched.
3
Dm7
A7♭9
6fr
Dm7
I nev - er thought my heart

Dm7
E♭dim7
Em7
B7♭9
E7♭9
could be had
but now I'm caught and I'm
Am
Dm7
Dm7/G
kind - a glad to be
be -
1
C6
A♭13
G13
C♯dim7
Dm7
witched.
Be - witched
2
C6
G7♯5
C6
witched.

BONANZA

Theme from the TV Series

Words and Music by JAY LIVINGSTON and RAY EVANS

C
We're not a one to sad - dle up and run, bo - nan - za!
G7sus
G7
An - y - one of us who starts a lit - tle fuss
Dm7/G
G7
C
knows he can count on me!
G
C
G/D
A9
One for four four for one, this we guar - an -

D9
G
tee!
We got a right to pick a lit - tle fight, bo -
nan - za!
D7sus
If an - y - one fights
D7
an - y - one of us,
Am7/D
D7
he's got - ta fight with
G
me!
G
me!
f
f

BUBBLES IN THE WINE

featured in the Television Series THE LAWRENCE WELK SHOW

Words and Music by FRANK LOESSER,
BOB CALAME and LAWRENCE WELK

C7
F6
Oh, may - be it's that moon, or may - be it's that tune, play - ing as we
F
D7
gen - tly sway; or may - be it's the fact that I love you.
Dm7/G
G7
C
Can't real - ly say, how I get this way. My heart whis - pers a re -
C/E
E♭dim7
Dm7
G7
frain, like bub - bles in the wine ev - 'ry time you're close to me.

C7
F6
I need - n't drink cham - pagne, a feel - ing quite in - sane lights me up and
F
Fm
sets me free. Some day I may lose you, but no mat - ter how fate may go, a -
C
Am7
D9
4fr
Dm7/G
G7
C
part or to - geth - er, when I think of to - night I know I'll hear in this heart of
Gm/B♭
A7
D7
Dm7/G
G9
1
C
E♭dim7
Dm7
G7
2
C
mine, mu - sic like the pret - ty bub - bles in the wine. My wine.

THE BRADY BUNCH

Theme from the Paramount Television Series THE BRADY BUNCH

Words and Music by SHERWOOD SCHWARTZ
and FRANK DEVOL

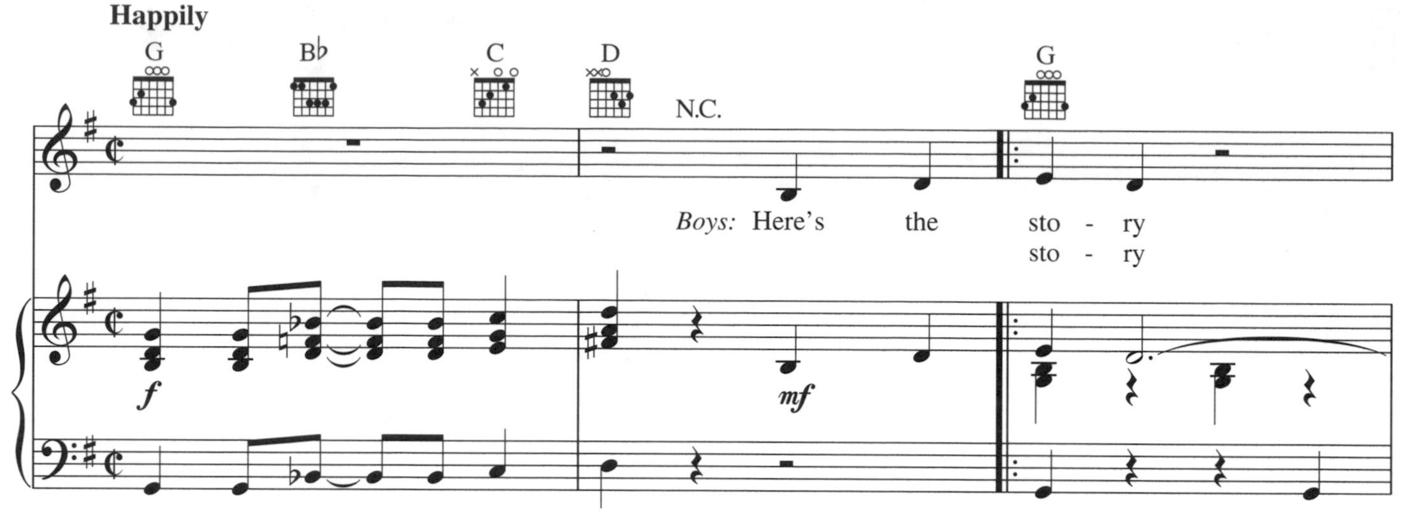

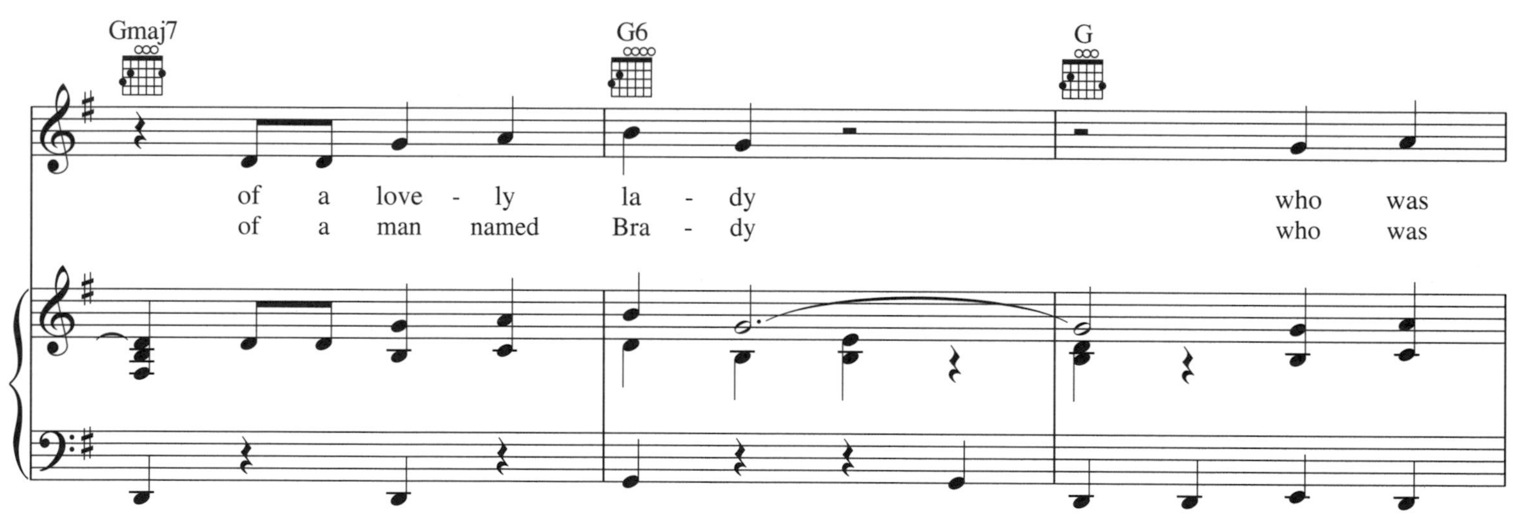

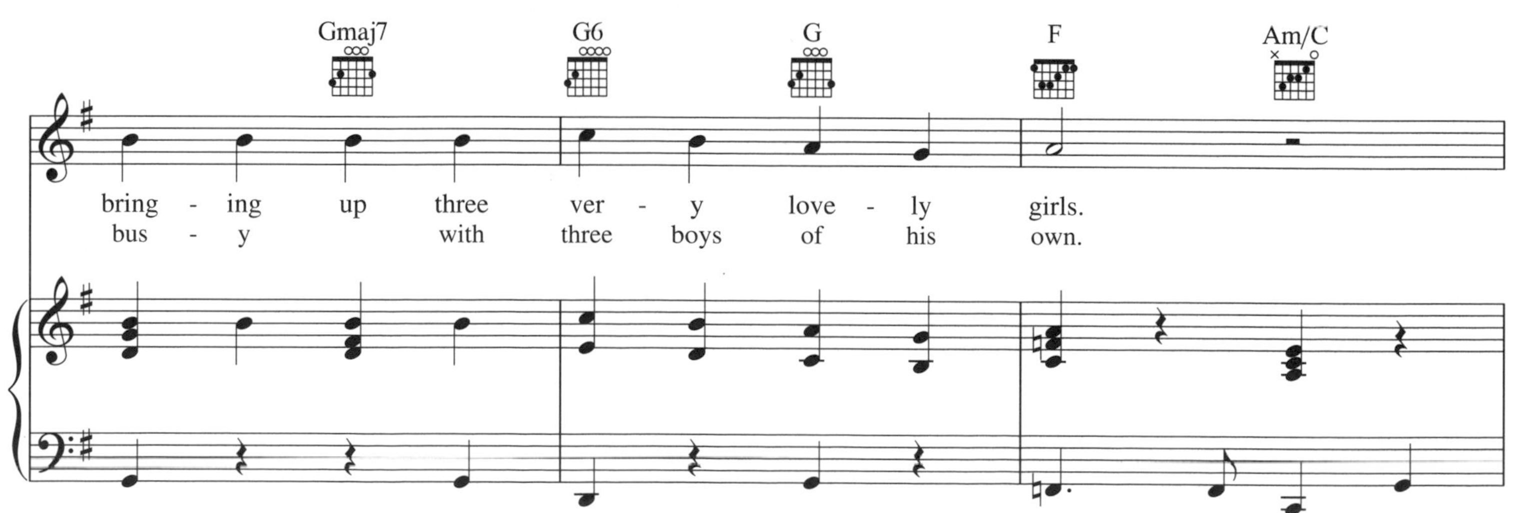

D7
Am7
D7
All of them had hair of gold
They were four men liv - ing all to -
Am7
D7
1
like their moth - er, the young - est
geth - er, yet they were
G
2
one in curls. Girls: It's the all a -
G
G7
C/G
G
E♭7
A♭
4fr
lone. All: 'Til the one day when the
f
mf

A♭maj7
A♭6
A♭
la - dy met this fel - low, and they
knew that it was much more than a hunch
B♭m7
E♭
B♭m7
E♭7
that this group must some - how form a
B♭m7
E♭7
B♭m7
fam - 'ly. That's the way we all be -

Eb7
Ab
4fr
came the Bra - dy Bunch. The Bra - dy
Db
Db7
Gb/Db
Db
Ab
Ab7
Db/Ab
Ab
Bunch, the Bra - dy Bunch. That's the
Bb
Eb
3fr
Eb7
way we be - came the Bra - dy
Ab
Db/Ab
Ab
N.C.
Bunch.
f

"C" IS FOR COOKIE

Eb/Bb
Bb7
To Coda
1 Eb
no chord
2 Eb
no chord
cook - ie, cook - ie, cook - ie starts with C.
moon sometimes looks like a C,
C. (Spoken:) Hey, you know what?
3
D.S. al Coda
Eb
Bb7
no chord
but you can't eat that. So
CODA
Eb
Eb/Bb
Bb7
C. Yeah! Cook - ie, cook - ie, cook - ie starts with
Eb
Eb/Bb
Bb7
Eb
C. Oh boy! Cook - ie, cook - ie, cook - ie starts with C.

CASPER THE FRIENDLY GHOST

from the Paramount Cartoon

Words by MACK DAVID
Music by JERRY LIVINGSTON

F
C
G7
C
al - ways says "Hel - lo," and he's real - ly glad to meet cha. Wher -
F
C
D7
G7
ev - er he may go, he's kind to ev - 'ry liv - ing crea - ture.
C
C#dim7
Grown - ups don't un - der - stand why chil - dren love him the most, but
Dm7
G7
C
Am
Dm7
G7
Cm
3fr
G7
C
kids all know that he loves them so, Cas - per the friend - ly ghost.
f
p

CHARLIE BROWN THEME

By VINCE GUARALDI

G7
C
D7
G
G7
C
C♯dim
G
C♯dim
G/D
C♯dim
A7
D7
G
To Coda
G7
Cmaj7
3

D7
G
G7
C
Cdim
G/D
Cdim
G/D
C♯dim
A7
D7
G
D.C. al Coda
CODA
G
C♯dim
p–pp
G/D
C♯dim
1.
A7
D7
G
2.
A7
D7
G

CHRISTMAS TIME IS HERE

from A CHARLIE BROWN CHRISTMAS

Words by LEE MENDELSON
Music by VINCE GUARALDI

Db maj7
Gb13#11
Db maj7
Gb13#11
Sleigh-bells in the air, beau - ty ev - 'ry - where.
Am7
Eb9
D9
D7b9
Gm7
Db9
C13
C13b9
Yule - tide by the fire - side and joy - ful mem - 'ries there.
Fmaj9
Eb13#11
Fmaj9
E13#11
Christ - mas time is here, we'll be draw - ing near.
To Coda
Bm7b5
Bbm7
Am7
Abm7
Gm7
Bb/C
Fmaj9
Oh, that we could al - ways see such spir - it through the year.

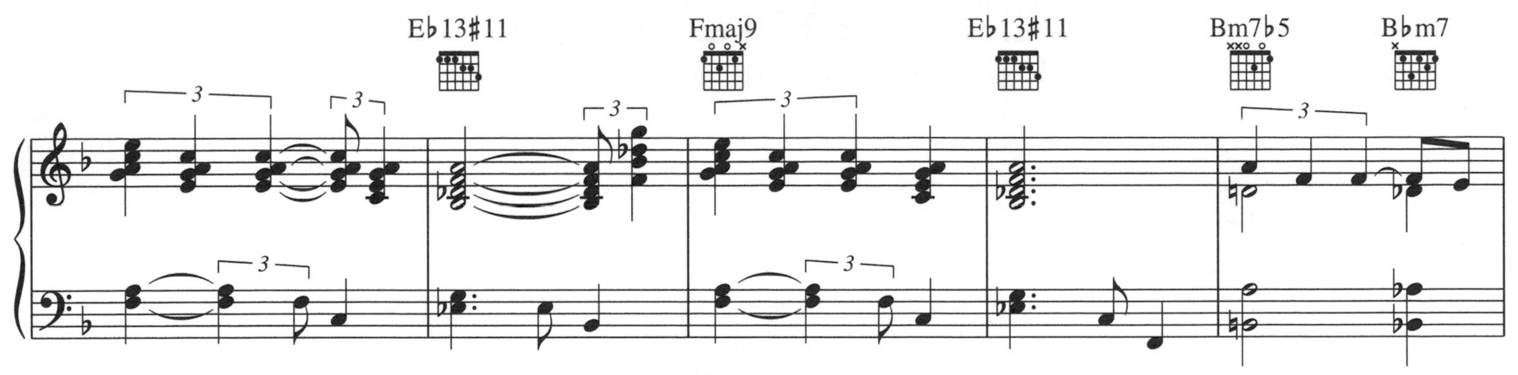

E♭13♯11
Fmaj9
E♭13♯11
Bm7♭5
B♭m7

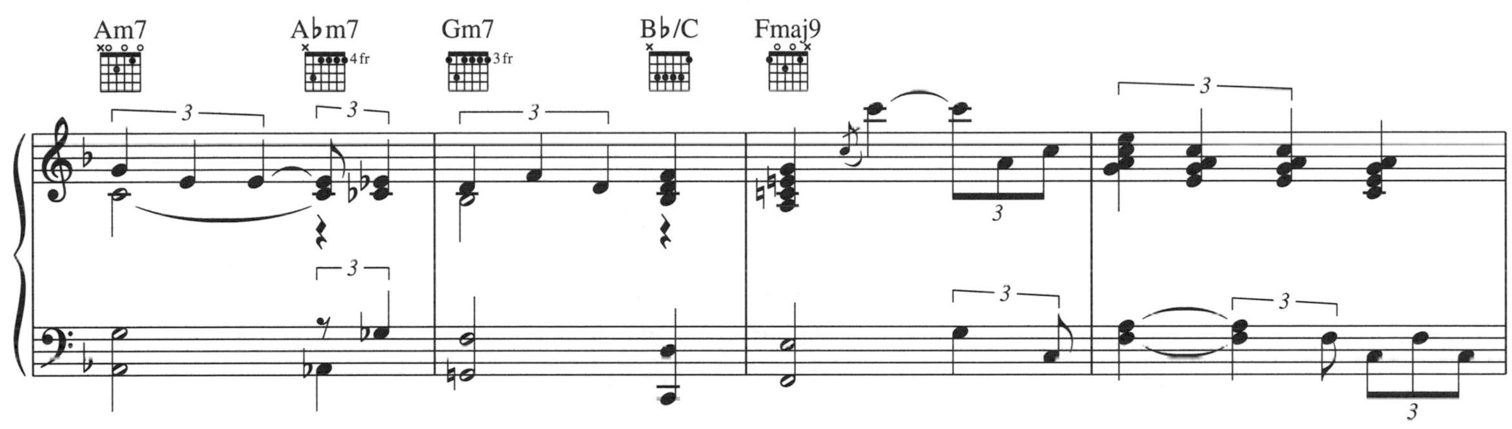

Am7
A♭m7
4 fr
Gm7
3 fr
B♭/C
Fmaj9

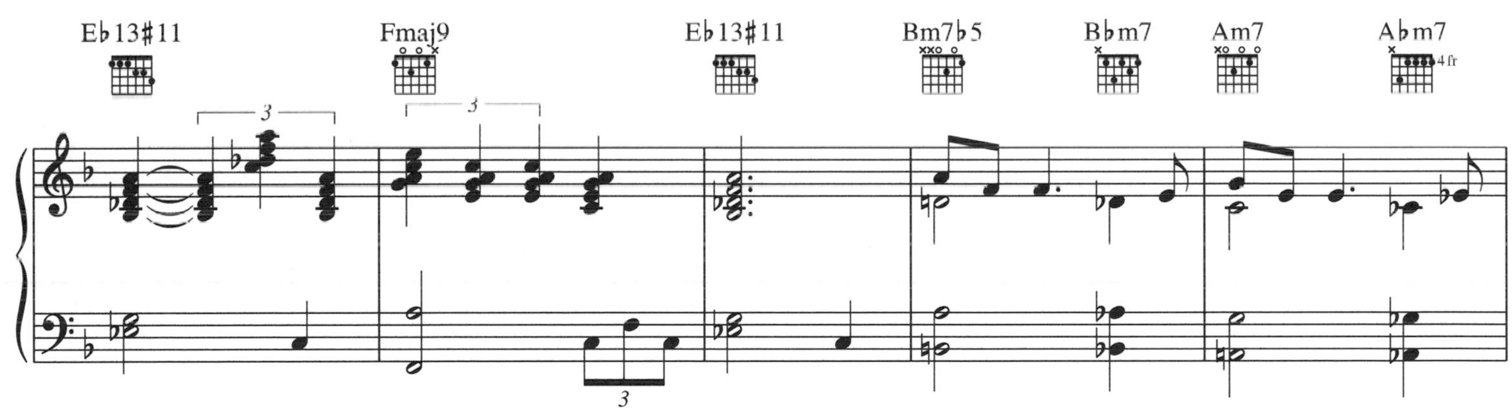

E♭13♯11
Fmaj9
E♭13♯11
Bm7♭5
B♭m7
Am7
A♭m7
4 fr

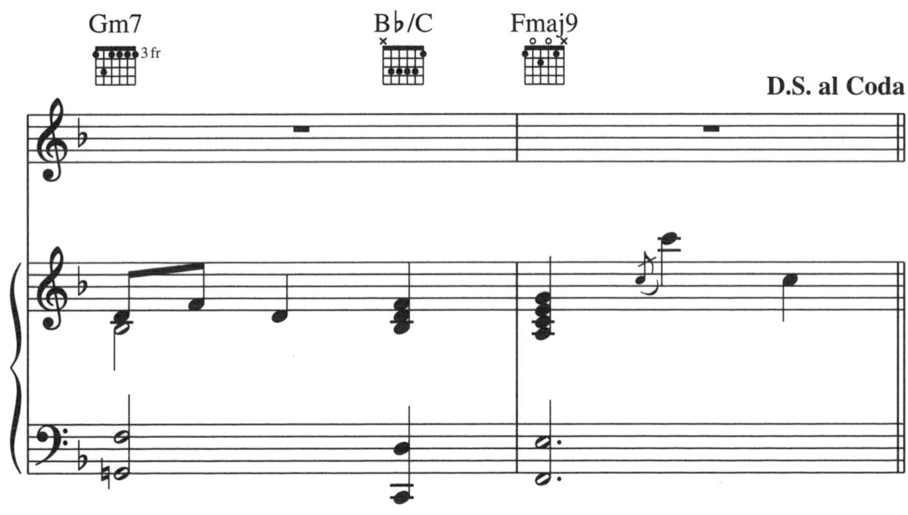

Gm7
3 fr
B♭/C
Fmaj9
D.S. al Coda

CODA
Fmaj9
year.

CLEVELAND ROCKS

Theme from THE DREW CAREY SHOW

Words and Music by
IAN HUNTER

D♭5
4fr
All the lit - tle chicks with the crim - son lips go,
A♭5
4fr
"Cleve - land rocks, Cleve - land rocks." She's liv - in' in sin with a
D♭5
4fr
safe - ty pin go - in', "Cleve - land rocks,
A♭
4fr
Cleve - land rocks,
B♭/A♭
D♭/A♭
4fr
Cleve - land rocks."
A♭5
4fr
A♭
4fr
Spoken: Ohio.

CLOSER TO FREE

from PARTY OF FIVE

Words and Music by SAM LLANAS
and KURT NEUMANN

G
C
D
Ev - 'ry - bod - y wants to be
Ev - 'ry - bod - y wants to be
C
G
C
To Coda
clos - er to free.
clos - er to free.
D
C
G
Ev - 'ry - bod - y
Instrumental solo
C
D
C
wants re - spect, just a lit - tle bit. And

G
C
D
ev - 'ry - bod - y needs a chance once in a while.
C
G
C
Ev - 'ry - bod - y wants to
D
C
G
be clos - er to free.
C
D
C
Solo ends

C(add9)
D
C(add9)
Ev - 'ry - bod - y one, ev - 'ry - bod - y
D
C(add9)
D
two, ev - 'ry - bod - y free.
1
2
D.S. al Coda
CODA
D
C
Yeah, clos - er to

G
C
D
free,
yeah,
C
G
C
clos - er to free,
D
C
G
clos - er to free.
C
D
C

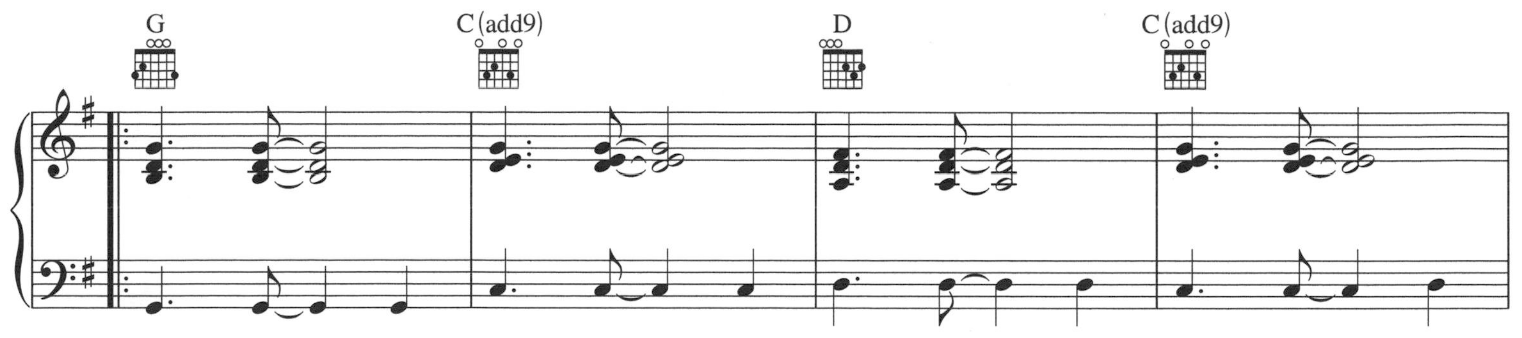
G
C(add9)
D
C(add9)

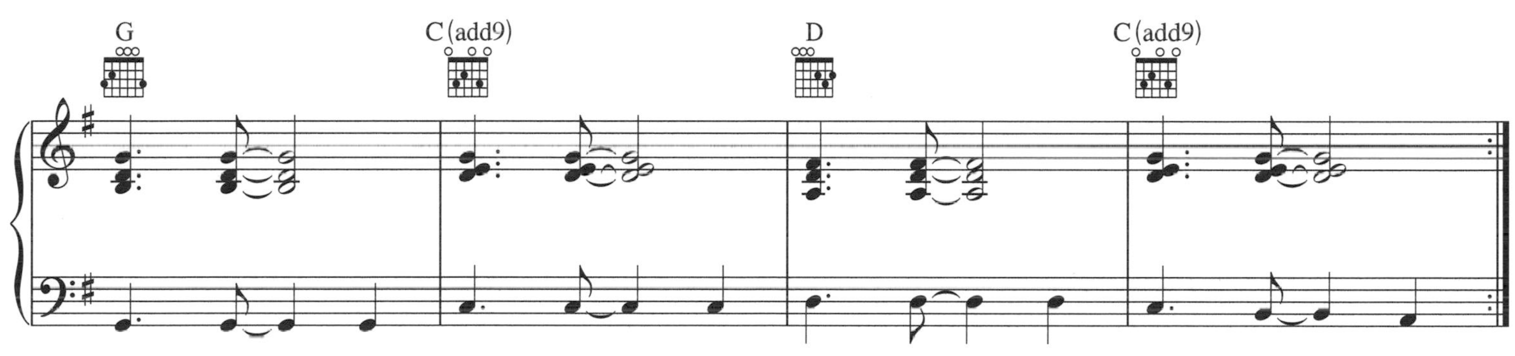
G
C(add9)
D
C(add9)

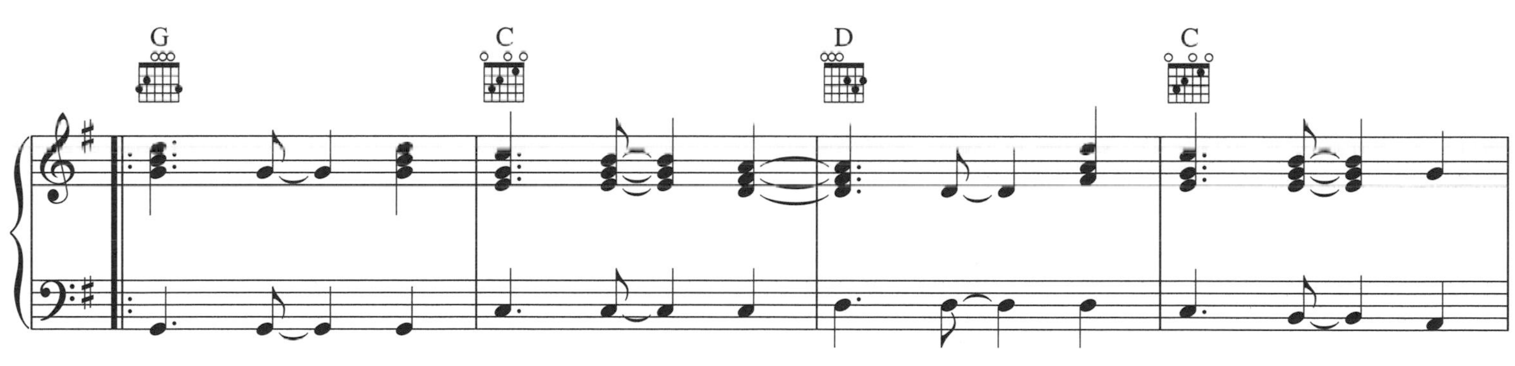
G
C
D
C

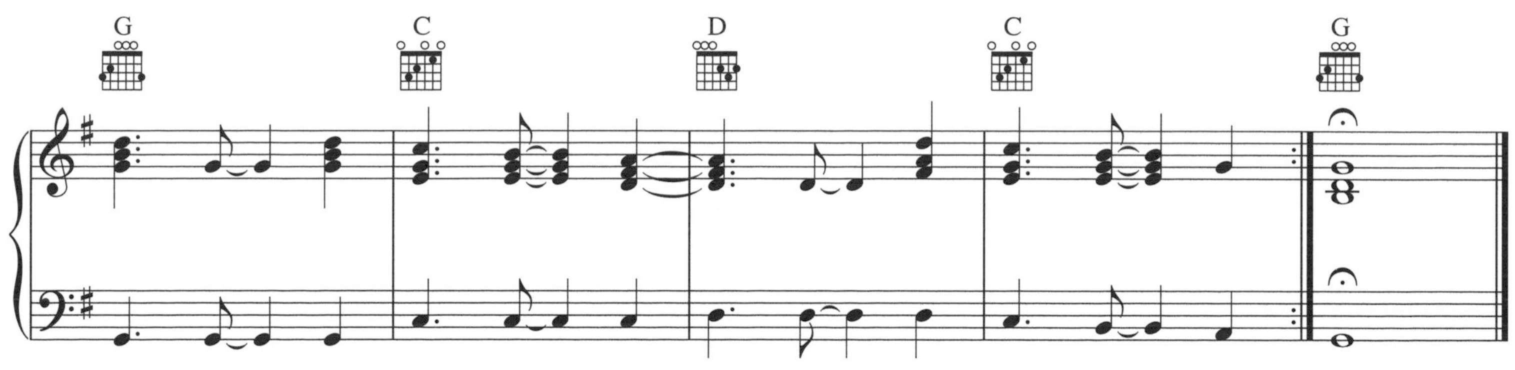
G
C
D
C
G

COME ON GET HAPPY

Theme from THE PARTRIDGE FAMILY

Words and Music by WES FARRELL
and DANNY JANSSEN

E♭ B♭ F E♭ Gm
3 fr
py. We had a dream we'd go
C E♭ B♭
trav-elin' to-geth - er we'd spread a lit - tle lov - in' then we'd keep mov - in' on.
Gm C E♭
Some-thin' al-ways hap-pens when-ev - er we're to-geth-er, we get a hap-py feel-in' when we're
B♭ B♭ F E♭
sing - in' a song. Trav-elin' a - long there's a song that we're sing - in',

B♭
F
E♭
3 fr
B♭
F
E♭
B♭
F
E♭
come on get hap - py.
A
whole lot of lov - in' is what we'll be bring - in',
we'll make you hap -
- py,
we'll make you hap - py,
we'll make you hap - py.

DAY BY DAY

Theme from the Paramount Television Series DAY BY DAY

Words and Music by SAMMY CAHN,
AXEL STORDAHL and PAUL WESTON

B7
Em
Em (maj7)
Em7
end to my de - vo - tion; it's
A7
Em7
A7
Am7/D
deep - er, dear, by far than an - y o - cean.
D7♭9
4fr
E7♭9
Am7
I find that day by day you're mak - ing
D7
G
all my dreams come true. So come what may

Bm7♭5
E7
I want you to know
I'm
Am7
D7
G
Bm7♭5/F
yours a - lone
and I'm in love to
E7
E7♭9
Am7
D9
D7♭9
4fr
stay, as we go through the years, day by
1
G6
Am7
D9
2
G6
C
G
day.
day.
rall.

COME WITH ME NOW

Theme from LIFESTYLES OF THE RICH & FAMOUS

Words and Music by NORMAN GIMBEL
and BILL CONTI

Em
Am
Am/G
D7/F♯
F/G
1
2
Fmaj7
Em
C/E
Am
C+/G♯
C/G

Fmaj7
Dm7
F/G
C
3
Dm/C
3
Dm/G

Come with me now and bring all your dreams,
Buccaneer ships and conquering schemes to me.
I'll hoist your sail and steer you through the darkness.
I'll be your friend and take you safely through.

You have the right to walk on a star,
Fly past the sun to galaxies far beyond.
I'll chart your way and lead you through the sunsets.
I'll be your friend and speed you safely there.

All that's unknown we'll dare it.
All that you face we'll share it.
All that you dream you can do now.
You'll get through.
We are two now.

Come with me now to what we've begun,
Love that will last as long as the sun will shine.

COURTSHIP OF EDDIE'S FATHER

from the Television Series

Words and Music by
HARRY NILSSON

B
Peo - ple, let me tell you a - bout him; he's so much fun, whether - er we're
talk - in' man to man or wheth - er we're talk - in' son to son 'cause he's my
best friend.
Yeah, he's my best friend.
A
D/E
A
Repeat and Fade
La la la la la la la la la la la la

DIFFERENT WORLDS

Theme from the Paramount Television Series ANGIE

Words NORMAN GIMBEL
Music by CHARLES FOX

A♭maj7
A♭/B♭
E♭maj7
3fr
Gm7
3fr
dif - f'rent worlds; drawn to each oth - er by the
A♭maj7
A♭/B♭
Gm7
3fr
Gm7/C
love in - side of us. We give to each oth - er our
Fmaj7
Em7
A7
dif - f'rent worlds. Long as we can do it,
Dmaj7
Dm7/G
G♭/A♭
4fr
life, we're gon - na breeze right thru it. Let the

D♭
Cm7♭5
F7
B♭m7
time flow, let the love grow, let the rain show'r, let the rose
G♭m
Fm7
B♭m7
Fm7
B♭m7
flow'r. Love, it seeks; love, it finds;
F♯m7
Bm7
2fr
Em7
Em7/A
love, it con - quers; love, it binds; love, it seeks, and love, it
F♯m7
Bm7
2fr
Em7
Em7/A
finds.
Love, it con - quers; love, it binds; love, it seeks and love, it

E♭maj7
3fr
Fm7
Gm7
3fr
finds.
Oo,
oo,
C9
Fm7
Fm7/B♭
oo.
F♯m7
Bm7
7fr
Em7
Em7/A
Love, it con - quers; love, it binds;
love, it seeks, and love, it
E♭maj7
3fr
Dmaj9♯11
4fr
finds.

DINOSAURS MAIN TITLE

from the Television Series

Music by
BRUCE BROUGHTON

Slightly faster, Bright Rag
A
mf
F#7
B7
E7
N.C.
A
F#7
B
E
A7
roughly
E7
A
F#m7
B9
E9
N.C.
A

DONNA REED THEME

from the Television Series

By WILLIAM LOOSE
and JOHN SEELY

D
Bm
Em7
A7
D(add9)
2 fr
Bm
Em7
A7
D
Bm
Em7
A7
F♯m7♭5
4 fr
B7
Em
Em7♭5
F♯m7
Bm7
2 fr
E13
Em7
A7
D6

DYNASTY THEME

from DYNASTY

By BILL CONTI

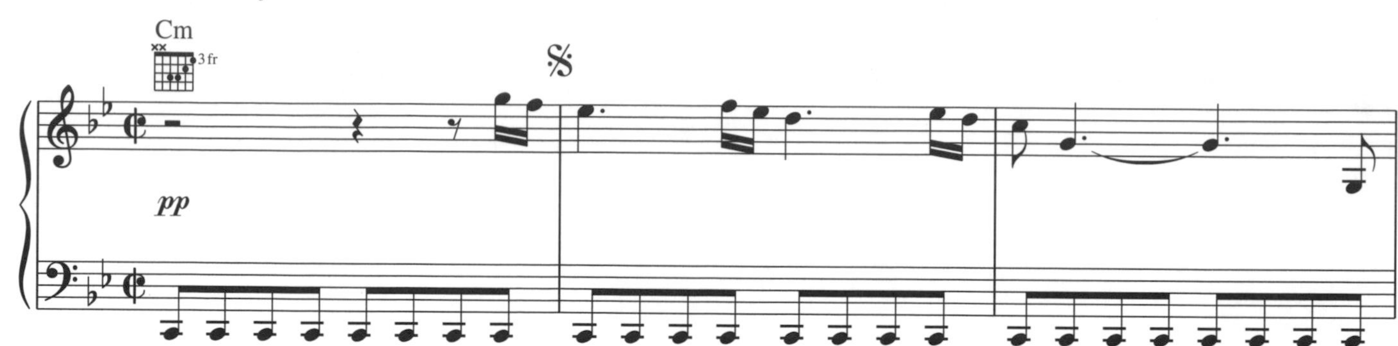

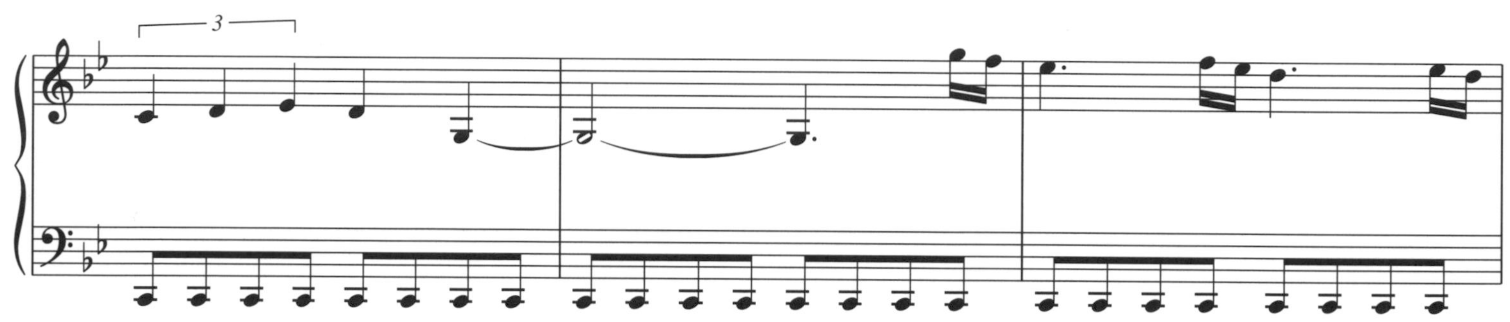

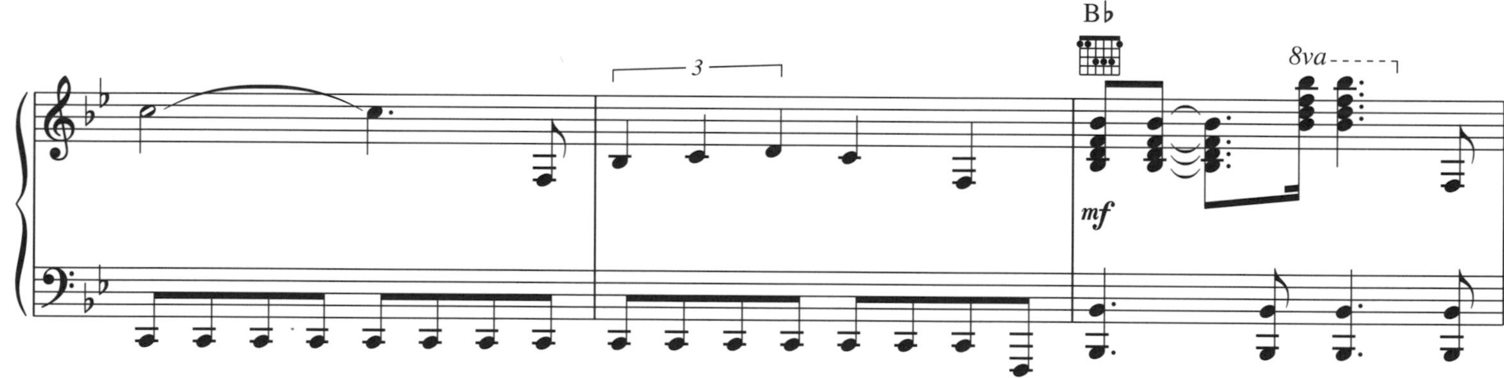

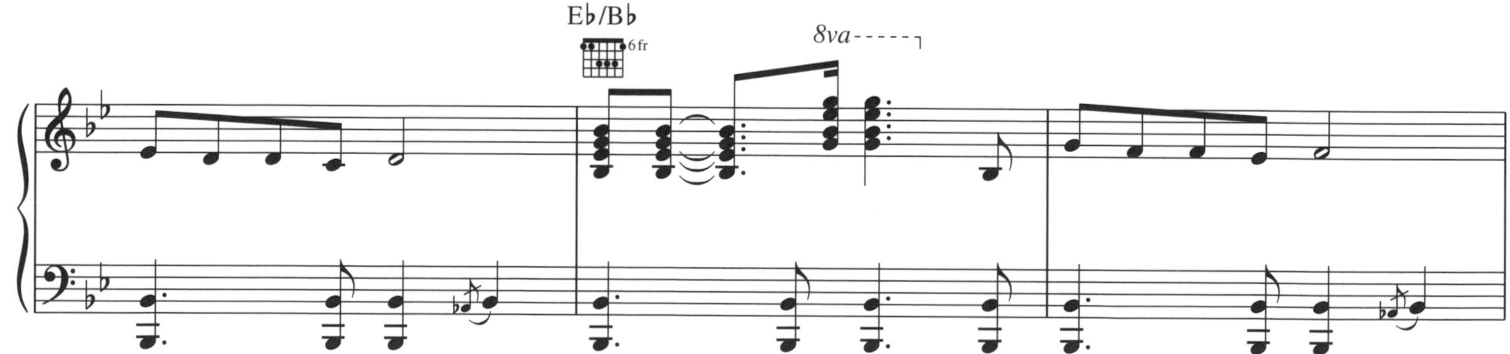

B♭
F
cresc.

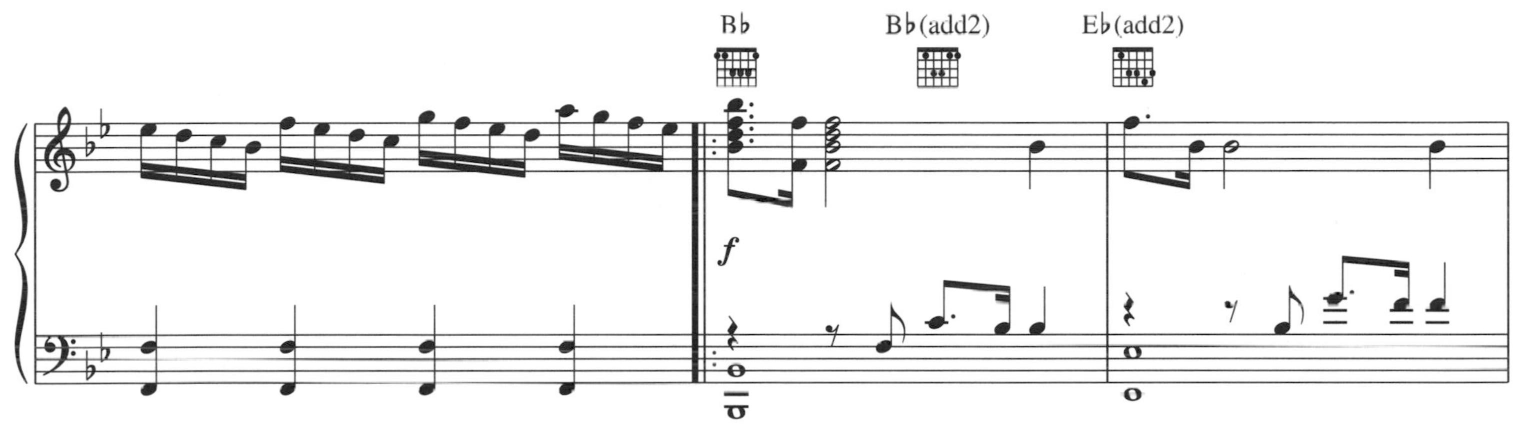
B♭
B♭(add2)
E♭(add2)
f

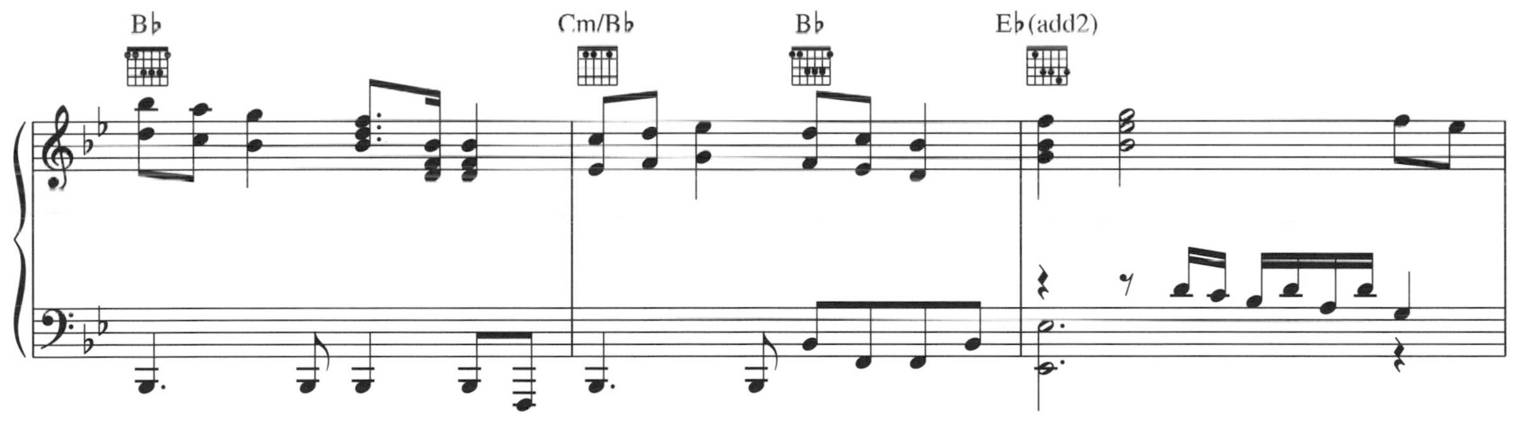
B♭
Cm/B♭
B♭
E♭(add2)

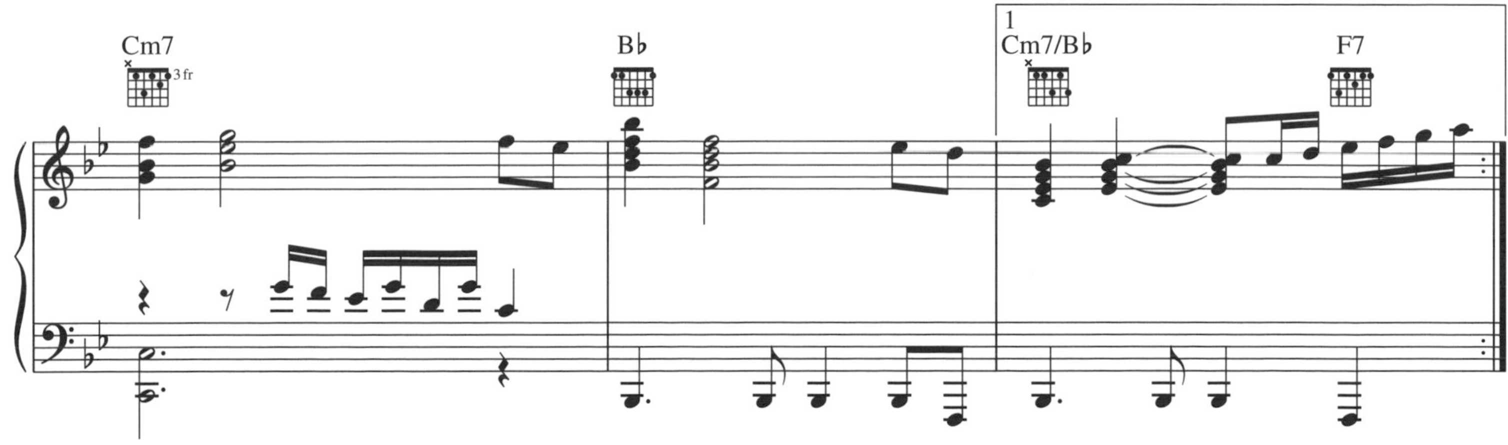
Cm7
3fr
B♭
1
Cm7/B♭
F7

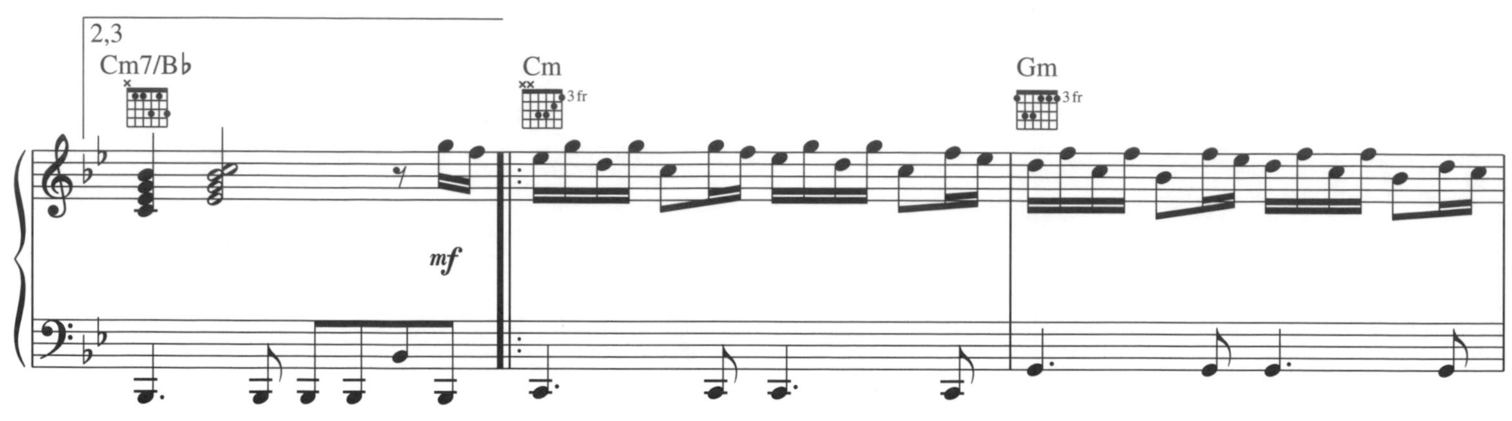
2,3
Cm7/B♭
Cm
3 fr
Gm
3 fr
mf

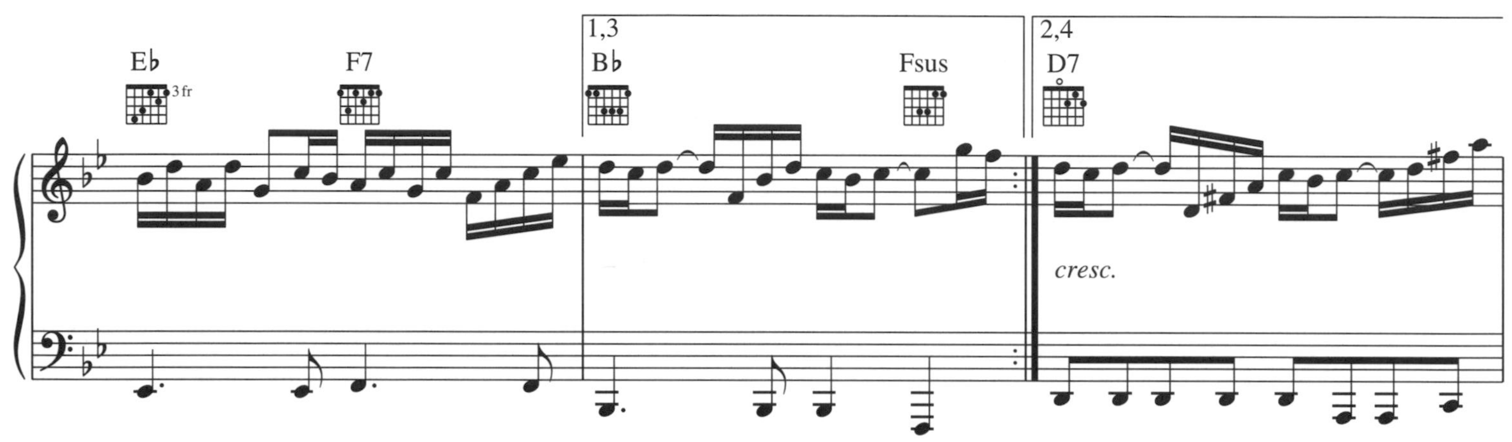
E♭
3 fr
F7
1,3
B♭
Fsus
2,4
D7
cresc.

B♭
B♭(add2)
E♭(add2)
B♭
8va
f

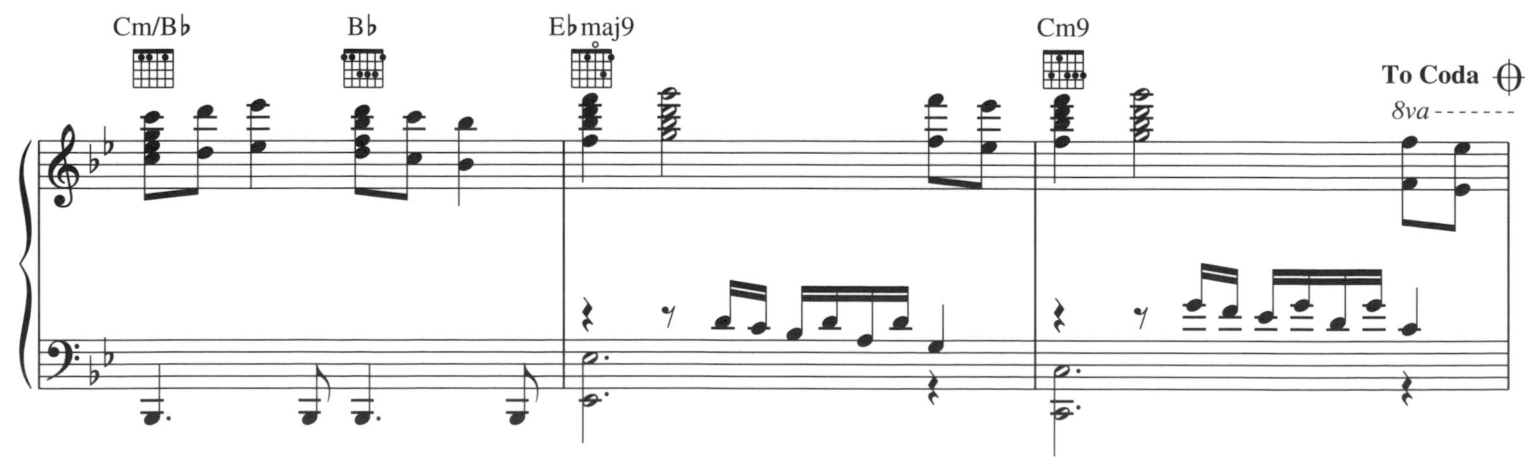
Cm/B♭
B♭
E♭maj9
Cm9
To Coda
8va

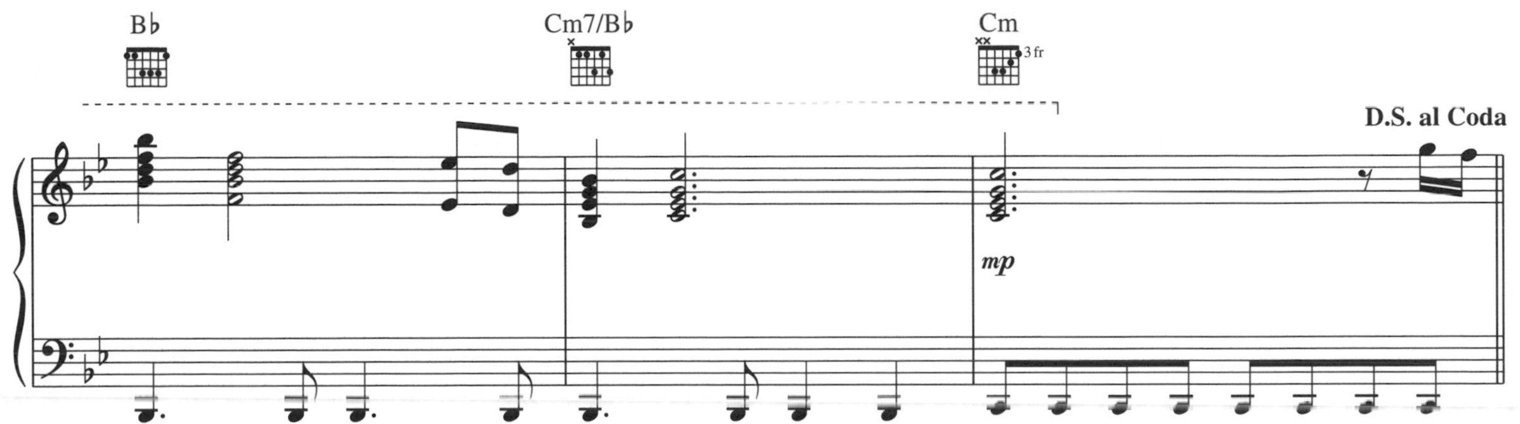
B♭
Cm7/B♭
Cm
3 fr
D.S. al Coda
mp

CODA
B♭
Cm/B♭
R.H. 8va to the end

B♭

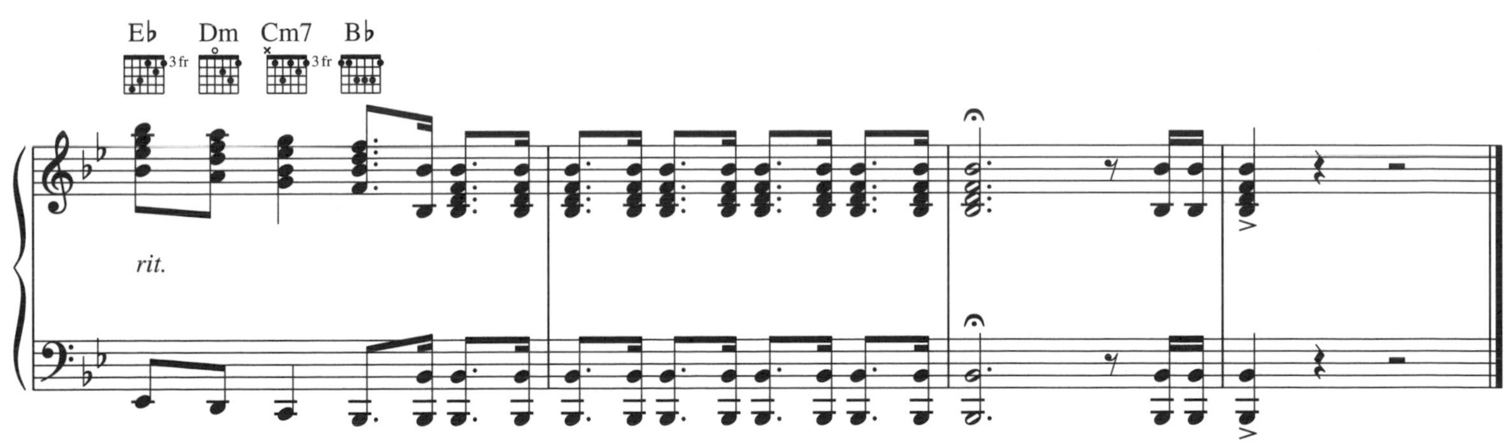
E♭
3 fr
Dm
Cm7
3 fr
B♭
rit.

ENTERTAINMENT TONIGHT

Theme from the Paramount Television Show

Music by MICHAEL MARK

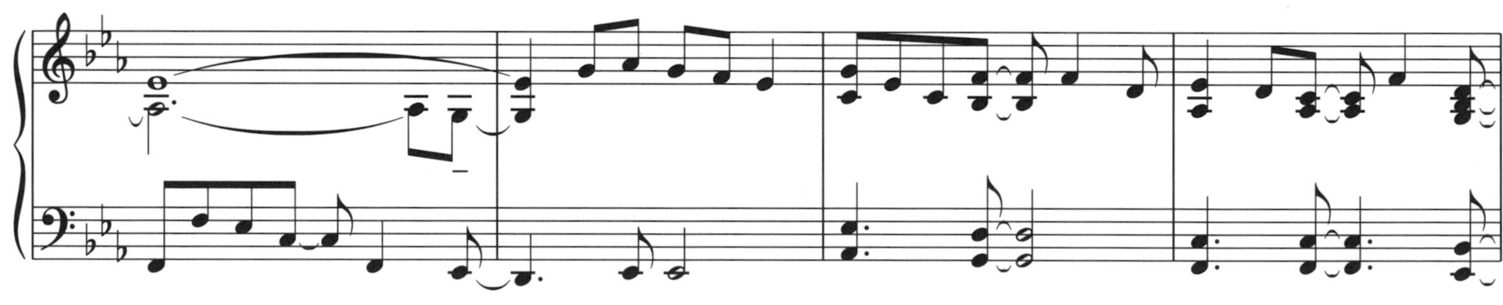

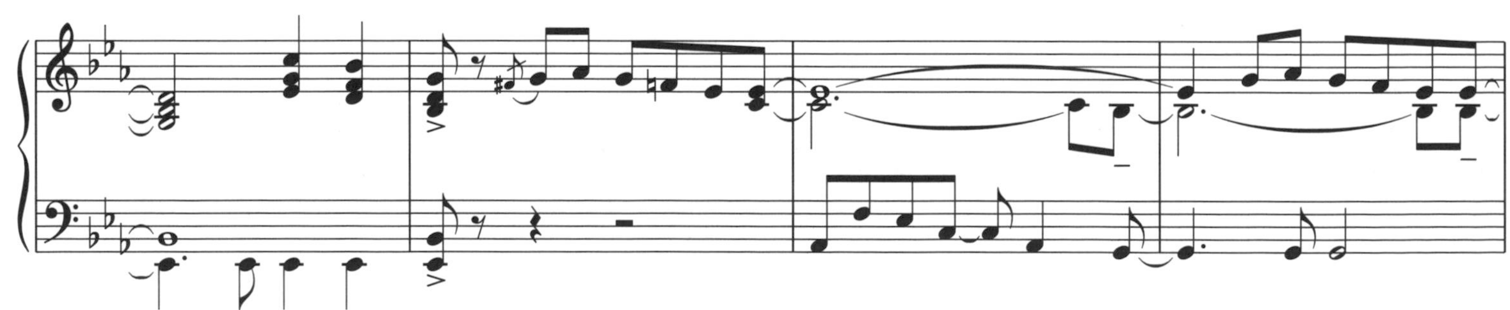

mp
3
mf
3
cresc.

f
mf

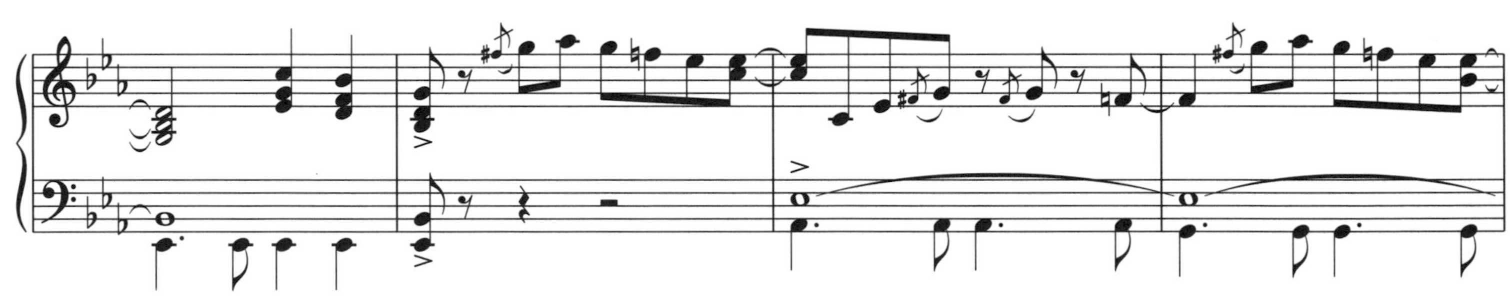

f
sffz

FELIX THE WONDERFUL CAT

from the Television Series

Words and Music by
WINSTON SHARPLES

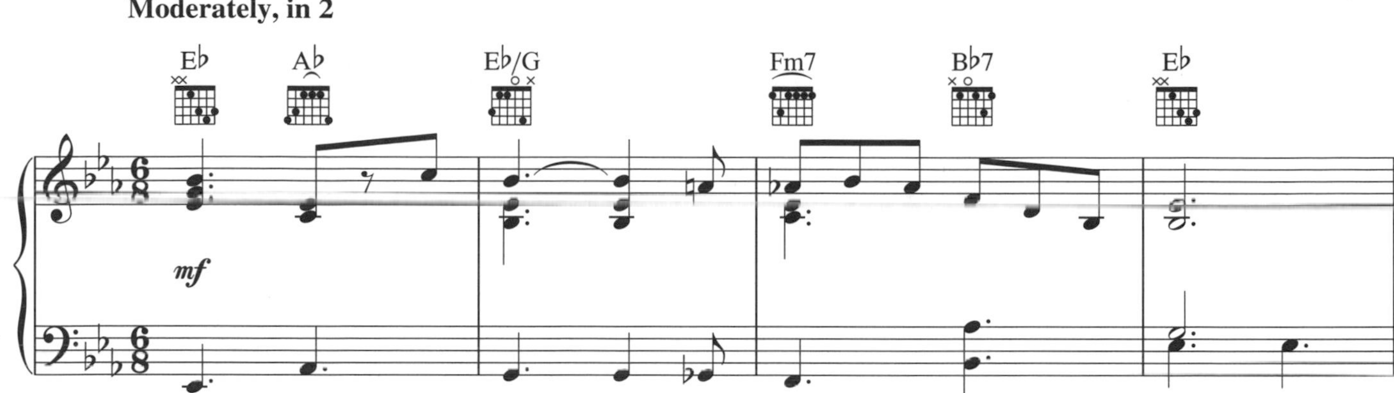

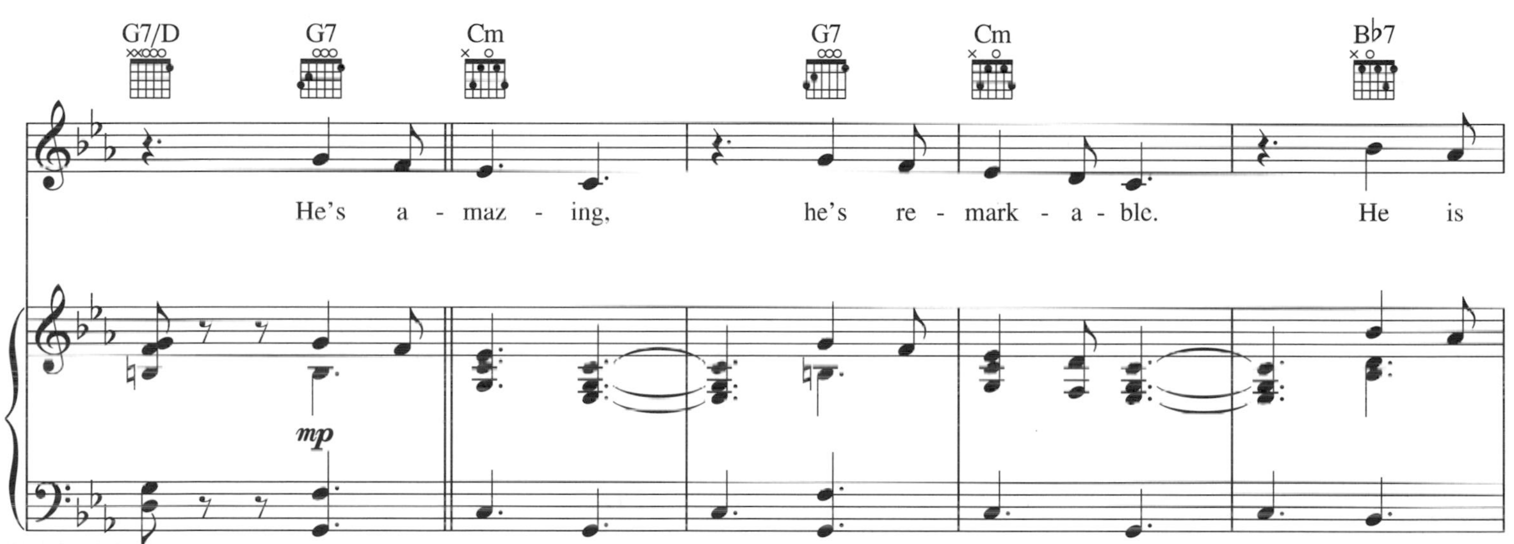

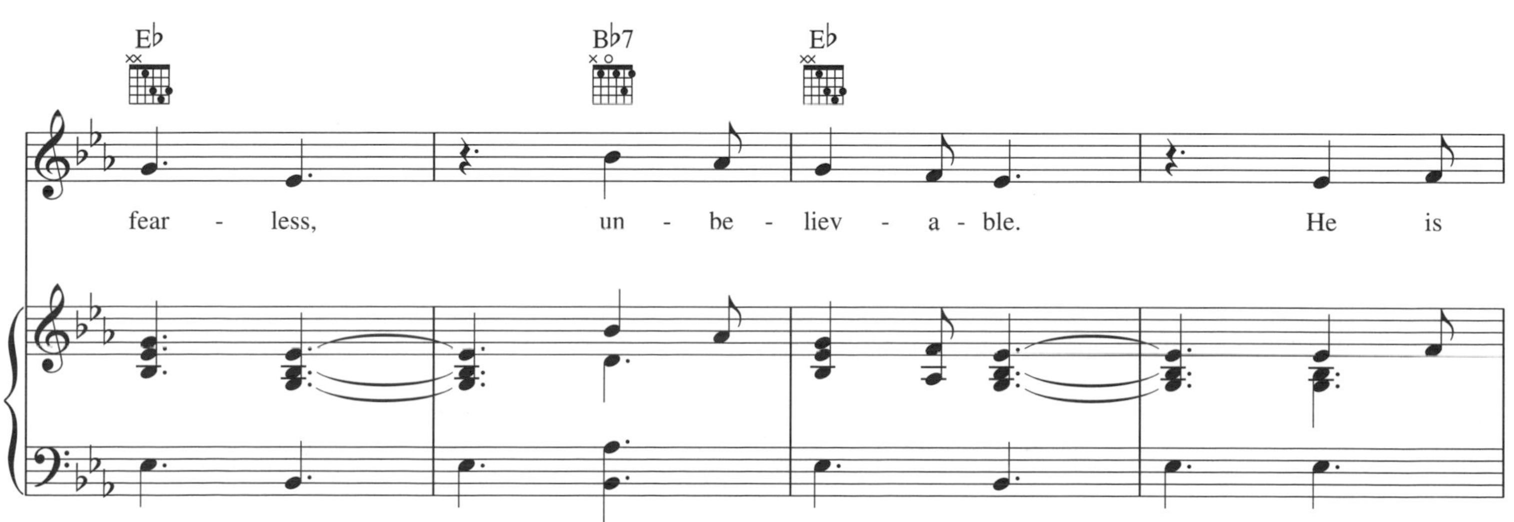

G7
Cm
su - per doo - per and ex - traor - di - nar - y.
He's the
F7
B♭
B♭9♯5
kind of guy that keeps you feel - ing mer - ry.
Who?
E♭
A♭
E♭/G
Fm7
B♭7
E♭
Fe - lix, the cat, the won - der - ful, won - der - ful cat.
When-
B♭7
E♭
F7
B♭7
ev - er he gets in a fix he reach - es in - to his bag of tricks.

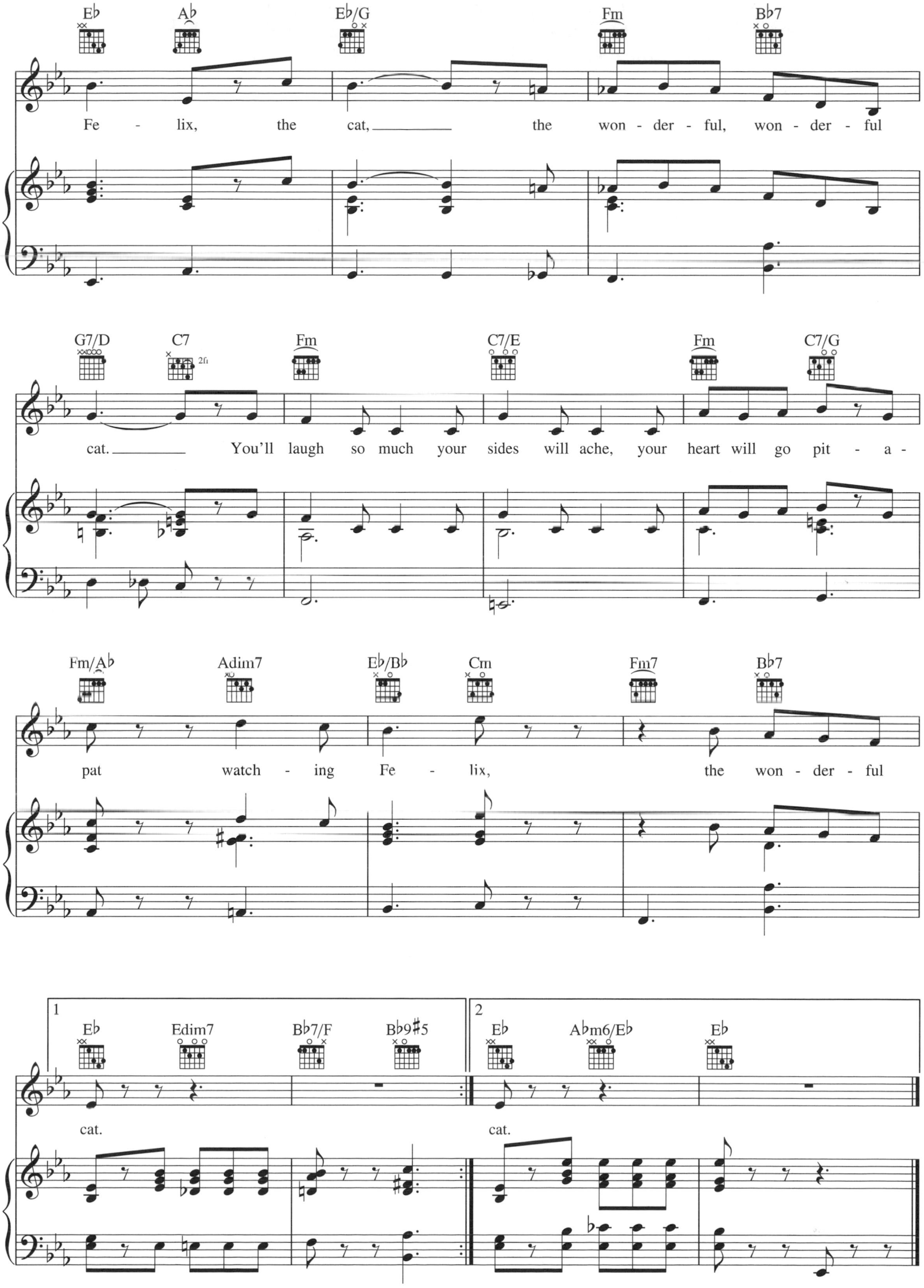

E♭ A♭ E♭/G Fm B♭7

Fe - lix, the cat, the won - der - ful, won - der - ful

G7/D C7 Fm C7/E Fm C7/G

cat. You'll laugh so much your sides will ache, your heart will go pit - a -

Fm/A♭ Adim7 E♭/B♭ Cm Fm7 B♭7

pat watch - ing Fe - lix, the won - der - ful

1 E♭ Edim7 B♭7/F B♭9♯5

cat.

2 E♭ A♭m6/E♭ E♭

cat.

FATHER KNOWS BEST THEME

from the Television Series FATHER KNOWS BEST

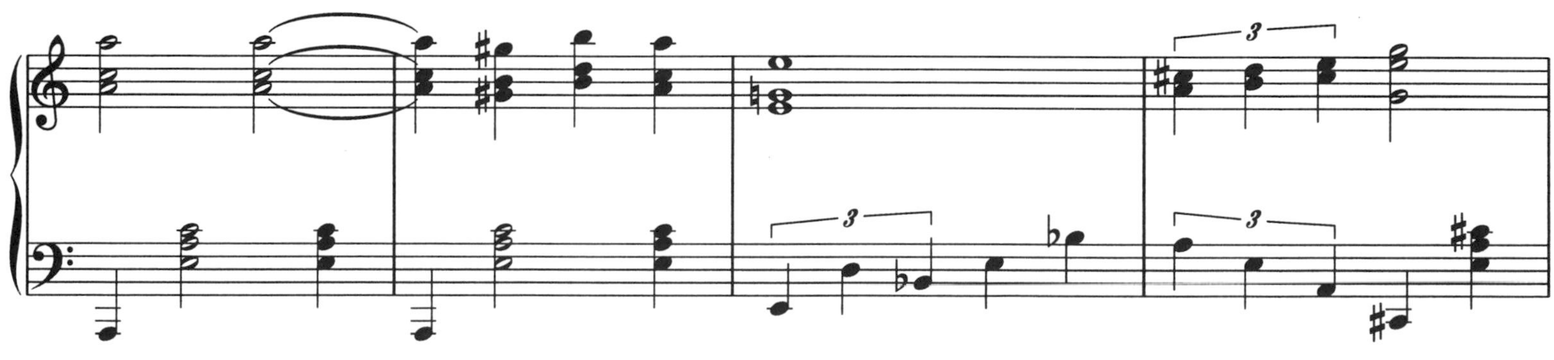

1
2

FRAGGLE ROCK THEME

from the Television Series

By PHILIP BALSAM
and DENNIS LEE

F7
Doo doo doo dee doo doo doo etc. (improvise words)
D
G
C
F
Hey! Dance your cares a - way,
G
C
F
G
F
C
wor - ry's for an - oth - er day.
Let the mu - sic play
down at Frag - gle Rock.

Hey look!
There goes a Fraggle!
Come on, let's get outa here!
8va
3rd time - optional improvisation
F
G

C
Eb
Bb
F
1,2
C
3
C
F
G
C
F
Dance your cares a-way, wor-ry's for an-oth-er day. Let the mu-sic play.
1,2
G
F
C
3
G
F
C
G
F
C
down at Frag-gle Rock, down at Frag-gle Rock, down at Frag-gle Rock,
G
F
C
down at Frag-gle Rock. Down at Fraggle Rock.

THEME FROM "FRASIER"

from the Paramount Television Series FRASIER

Words by DARRYL PHINNESSEE
Music by BRUCE MILLER

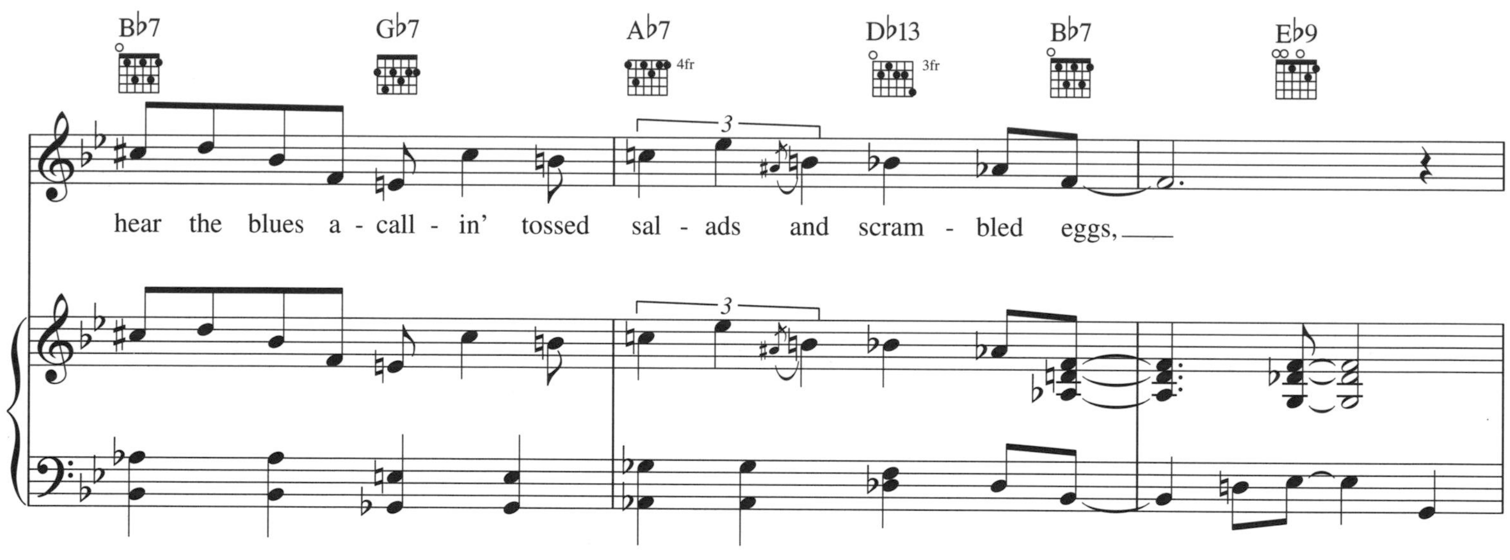

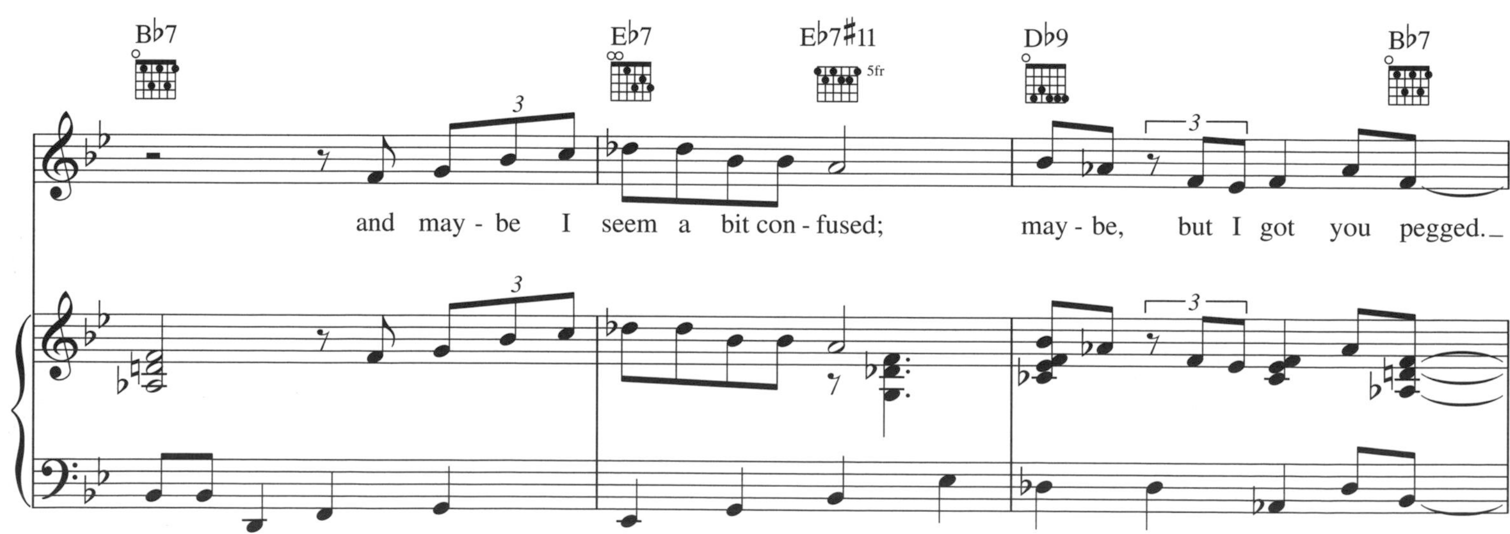

E♭9
B♭7
A7
A♭7
G7♯5
4fr
G♭7
F7
But I don't know what to do with those tossed
N.C.
F7♯9
sal - ads and scram - bled eggs.
They're call - in' a -
B♭7
E♭9
gain.
B♭7
E♭9
A♭13
3fr
A13♭9
2fr
B♭13
5fr
They're call - in' a - gain.

GEORGIA ON MY MIND

from the Television Series DESIGNING WOMEN

Words by STUART GORRELL
Music by HOAGY CARMICHAEL

A7 D7 D7♯5 D7 G9 C7
blos - soms fall and all the world's a song,
F A7♯5 A7/D Dm G7 Edim7 C13 F
2fr
I'll go back to Geor - gia 'cause that's where I be - long.
F A7 Dm
Geor - gia, Geor - gia, the whole day
Gm B♭m F E7 Gm G9 C7 F F♯dim
3fr 3fr
through. Just an old sweet song keeps Geor - gia on my mind.

Gm7
3fr
C7#5
F
A7
(Geor - gia on my mind.)
Geor - gia,
Geor - gia,
Dm
Gm
3fr
B♭m
F
E7
a song of you
comes as sweet and clear as
Gm
3fr
G9
C13
2fr
F
E♭9
F
A7
Dm
Gm6
3fr
moon - light through the pines.
Oth - er arms reach
Dm
B♭7
Dm
Gm6
3fr
Dm7
G7
out to me;
Oth - er eyes smile ten - der - ly;

Dm
Gm6
3fr
Dm7
E7
Am
F♯dim
Fm6
Still in peace - ful dreams I see the road leads back to
Dm
C7
F
A7
Dm
you. Geor - gia, Geor - gia, no peace I
Gm
Bbm
F
E7
Gm
G9
C13
3fr
find, Just an old sweet song keeps Geor - gia on my
1
F
Dm
Gm7
3fr
C13
2fr
C7♯5
mind.
2
F
Bb6/9
C7♯5
F6
mind.
rit.

GET SMART
from the Television Series

By IRVING SZATHMARY

Fm
D♭7
C7
Fm
D♭7
C7
Fm
D♭7
C7
Fm
D♭7
C7
C+
B+
B♭+
D♭7
Fm
D♭7
C7♭9
Fm
B♭m6
3
3
3
3

Gbm6
Bbm6
C7b9
Fm
Db7
C7
Fm
Db7
C7
Fm
Db7
C7
Fm
Db7
C7
C+
B+
Bb+
Db7
Fm
C7
Fm

HANDS OF TIME

Theme from the Screen Gems Television Production BRIAN'S SONG

Words by ALAN BERGMAN and MARILYN BERGMAN
Music by MICHEL LEGRAND

G
G/F#
C/E
D/F#
Hand in hand we'd choose the mo - ments that should
a tempo
Em6
Bm
Bm7
Em7
last; the love - ly mo - ments that should have no
A7sus4
A7
D
Dm7
fu - ture and no past. The sum-mer from the top of the
mf
Dmaj7
Dm7
Am7
swing, the com-fort in the sound of a lul - la - by, the

F
Amaj7
Am7/G
D/F#
in - no - cence of leaves in the spring, but most of all the mo - ment when
C/E
Am7/D
D
G
G/F#
C/E
D/F#
love first touched me! All the hap - py days would
rit.
a tempo
G
G/F#
F6
G7-9
Cmaj7
G/B
Em7
nev - er learn to fly, un - til the hands of time would choose to
Am7
D7
G
G/F#
C/E
Eb6
G
wave "good - bye."
rit.

THEME FROM "THE GREATEST AMERICAN HERO"

from the Television Series

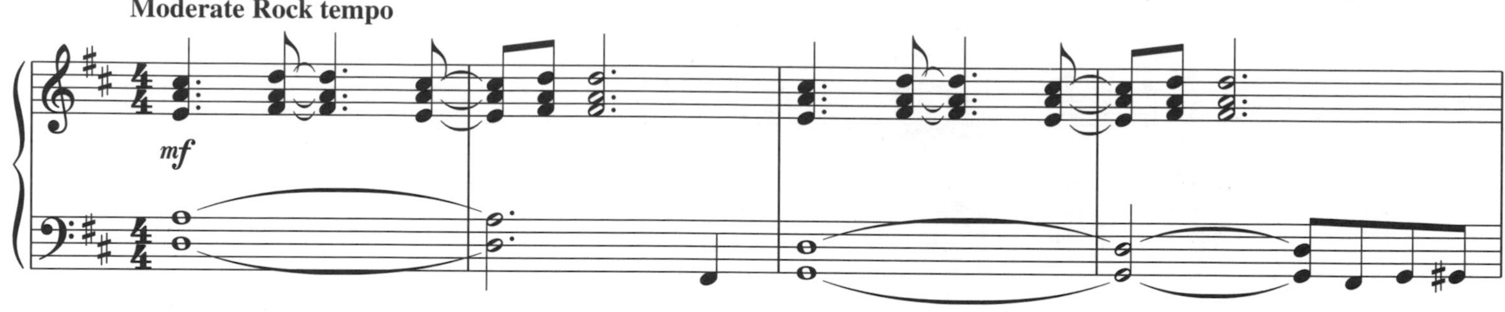

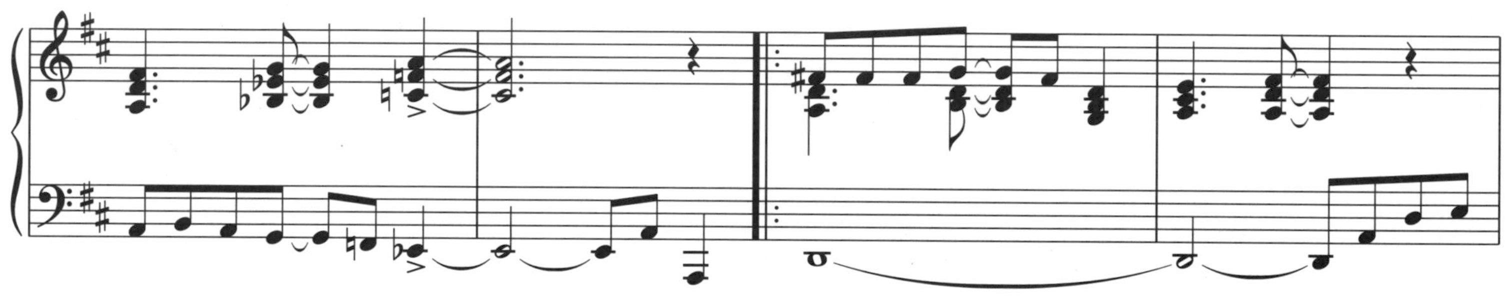

dim.

1.

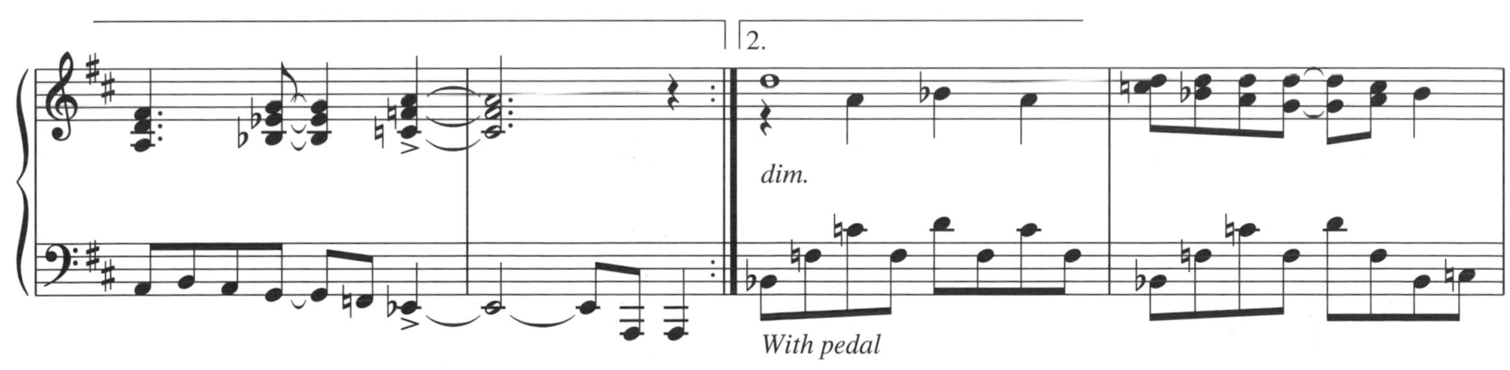
2.
dim.
With pedal

8va

cresc.
f

cresc.
rit.
mp

HAPPY DAYS

Theme from the Paramount Television Series HAPPY DAYS

Words by NORMAN GIMBEL
Music by CHARLES FOX

F
Dm
This day is ours.
B♭
C
F
Won't you be mine?
This day is ours.
Dm
B♭
C
Oh, please be mine.
F
Hel - lo, sun - shine, good - bye rain. She's

B♭
wear - ing my school ring on a chain.
G
She's my stead - y, I'm her man.
C
I'm gon - na love her all I can.
F
This day is ours.
Dm
B♭
C
Won't you be mine?

F
Dm
B♭
This day is ours.
Oh, please be mine.
C
F
Dm
These hap - py days are yours and mine.
B♭
C
These hap - py days are yours and mine,
B♭
B♭/C
F
hap - py days!
8vb.

HAPPY TRAILS

from the Television Series THE ROY ROGERS SHOW

Words and Music by
DALE EVANS

E♭
3fr
E♭
3fr
hap - py one for you. Hap - py trails to
Edim7
you until we meet a -
B♭7
B♭7sus
B♭7
gain. Hap - py trails to you, keep
B♭7♯5
E♭(add9)
E♭
3fr
smil - in' un - til then. Who

E♭7
A♭maj7
A♭6
3fr
cares a - bout the clouds when we're to - geth - er? Just
C7
F9
B♭7
sing a song and bring the sun - ny weath - er. Hap - py
E♭
3fr
B♭m6
6fr
C7
Fm
B♭7
trails to you till we meet a -
1
E♭
3fr
B♭7
gain. Hap - py
2
E♭
3fr
A♭
4fr
E♭6
gain.

HARLEM NOCTURNE

featured in the Television Series MIKE HAMMER

Words by DICK ROGERS
Music by EARLE HAGEN

Cm7
3fr
E♭7
D7
3
the dark - ness is taunt - ing me.
Gm6
3fr
N.C.
Gm6
3fr
Oh! what a sad re - frain,
Cm6
a noc - turne born in Har - lem.
Cm7
3fr
E♭7
D7
3
That mel - an - chol - y strain for - ev - er is haunt - ing me.

Gm6
3fr
C9
Gm6
3fr
G♭9
3fr
F9
B♭7
Fm7
B♭7
Fm7
The mel - o - dy clings a - round my heart strings, it
B♭7
Fm7
B♭7
B7
B♭7
won't let me go when I'm lone - ly. I
E♭7
B♭m7
E♭7
B♭m7
hear it in dreams and some - how it seems it

N.C.
makes me weep and I can't sleep. An
F7
Bb7
Fm7
Bb7
Fm7
Bb7
Fm7
in - di - go tune, it sings to the moon the lone-some re - frain of a
Bb7
B7
Bb7
Eb7
Bbm7
Eb7
Bbm7
lov - er. The mel - o - dy sighs, it laughs and it cries a
N.C.
moan in blue that wails the long night

Gm6
D7♯5
Gm6
N.C.
Gm6
thru.
Tho' with the dawn it's gone,
Cm6
the mel - o - dy lives ev - er
for lone - ly hearts to learn
Cm7
E♭7
D7
Gm6
Cm6
of love in a Har - lem Noc - turne.
Gm6
Cm6
Gm
D7
Gm (add9)
C13
Gm (add9)
3fr
2fr
molto rit.

HEAVEN

Theme from the Television Show HIGHWAY TO HEAVEN

Music by
DAVID ROSE

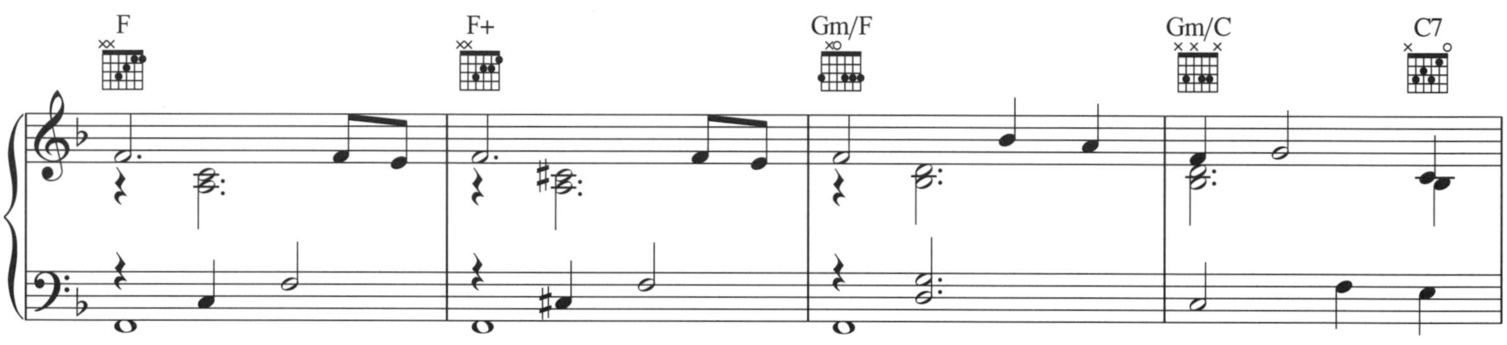

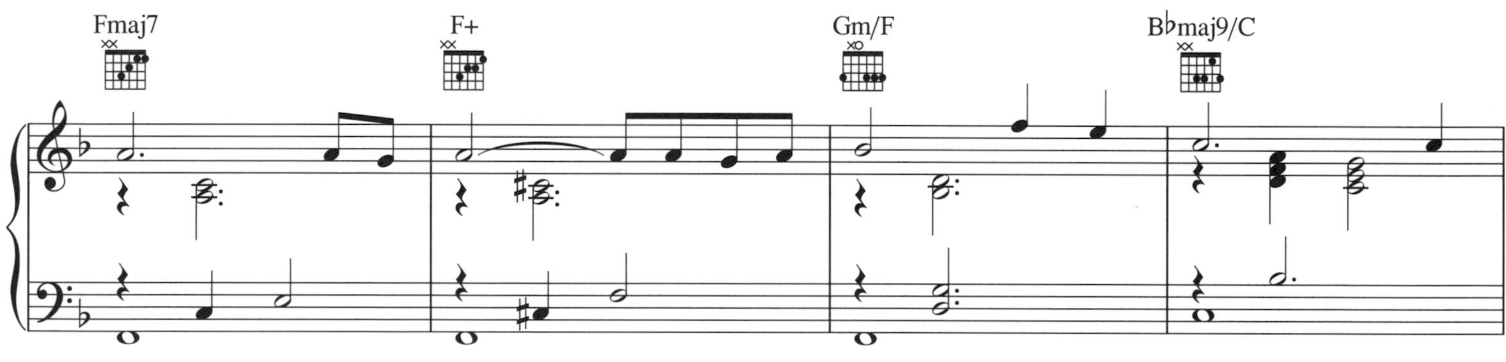

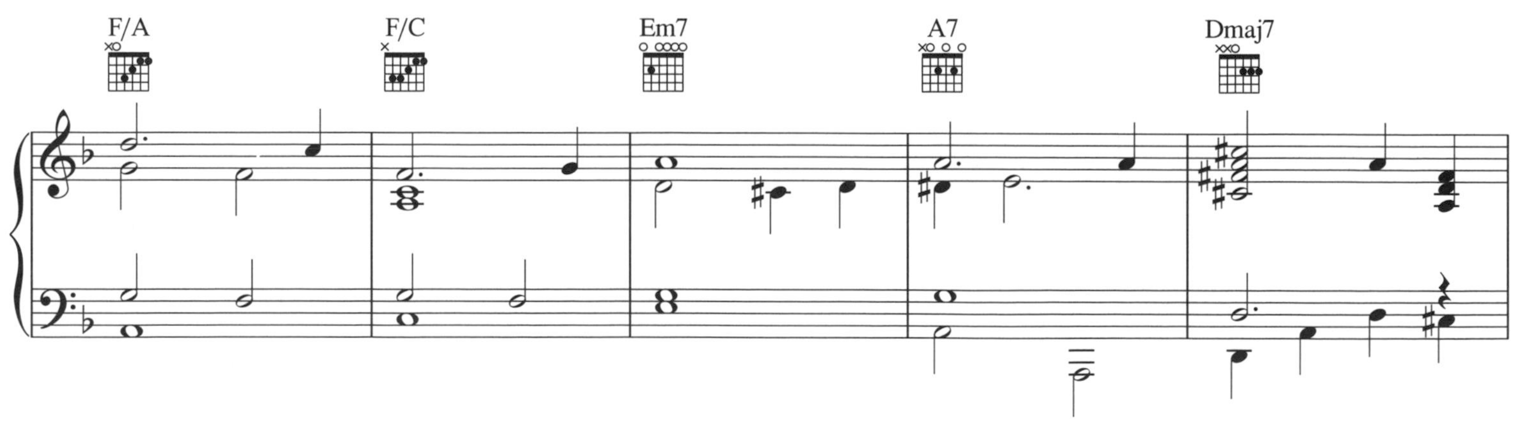

Bm
Bm/A
Gm7
B♭m6/C
C7
F
F+
B♭/F
Gm7/C
C7
F
F7♯5
Gm/F
B♭maj9/C
C7
E♭maj7/F
B♭maj9
B♭m6
F/C
Gm/C
F/C
D♭+/C
2fr
Gdim/C
2fr
D♭+/C
2fr
B♭maj7/C
C7
F
E♭
3fr
F

HOME IMPROVEMENT

Theme from the TV Series

Music by DAN FOLIART

G
A
E
G
A
N.C.
E
F7
A♭
B♭
F7
A♭
B♭
F7
A♭
B♭
N.C.
F9
E9
E♭9
D9
D♭
E♭
F
mf
ff

I DON'T WANT TO WAIT

featured in DAWSON'S CREEK

Words and Music by
PAULA COLE

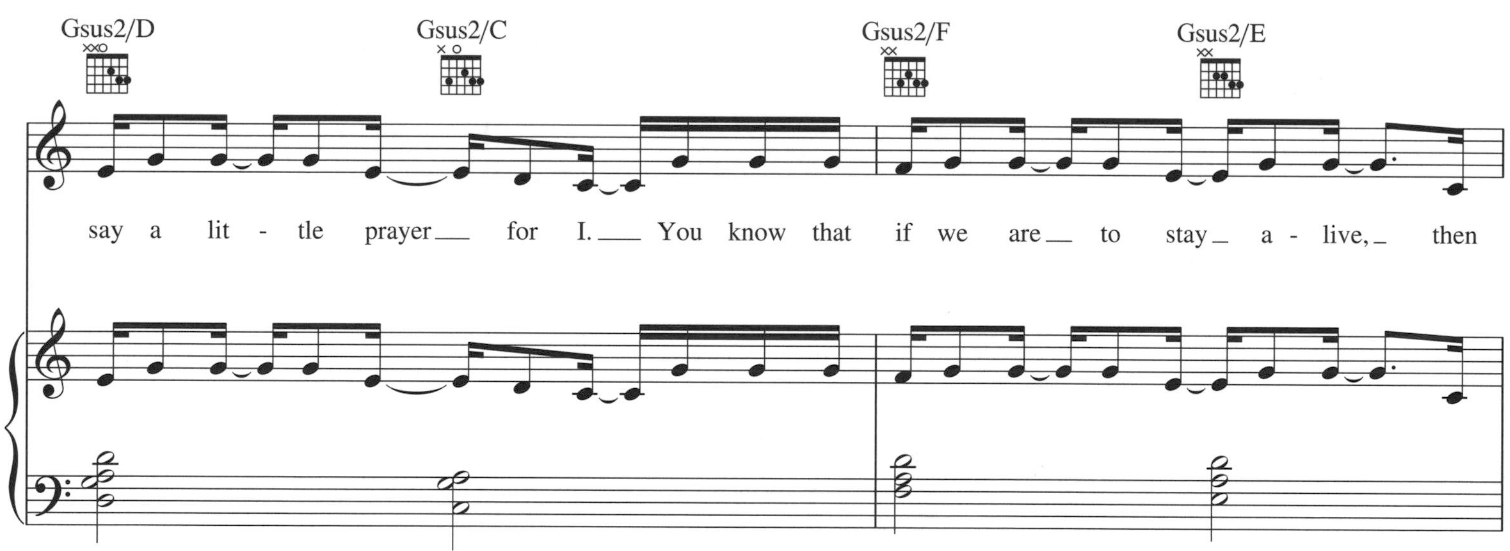

C6/9
du du du du du,
du du du du du du.
G(add2)
She had two ba - bies,
He showed up all wet
C6/9
one was six months, one was three,
on the rain - y front step
in the war of for - ty - four.
wear - ing shrap - nel in his skin.
G(add2)
Ev - 'ry tel - e - phone ring,
And the war he saw
ev - 'ry heart - beat sting - ing when she
lives in - side him still. It's so

Em7
D
Cmaj9
thought it was God calling her. Oh, would
hard to be gen - tle and warm. The years
Em
D6
C(add9)
her son grow to know his fa - ther?
pass by, and now he has grand - daugh - ters.
G(add2)
D(add4)/F#
Em11
7fr
Dsus
I don't want to wait for our lives to be o - ver. I want
C6
G(add9)/B
Dsus/A
Dsus
to know right now, what will it be?

G(add2)
D(add4)/F♯
Em11
7fr
Dsus
I don't want to wait for our lives to be o - ver. Will it
C6
G(add9)/B
1
Dsus/A
G(add2)
be yes, or will it be sor - ry? Du du du du du,
C6/9
du du du du du, du du du du du du.
2
Dsus/A
G7(add4)
Oh, so you look at me from a - cross

Am9♭13
the room. You're wear - ing your an - guish a - gain. Be - lieve
B♭(add2)
Fsus
C(add9)
me, I know the feel - ing; it sucks you in - to the jaws of an - ger.
G7(add4)
Oh, so breathe a lit - tle more deep - ly, my love. All we
Am9♭13
B♭(add2)
have is this ver - y mo - ment, and I don't want to do what his fa - ther and his fa - ther and

Fsus
Gsus2
his fa - ther did. I want to be here now.
So
Gsus2/F
Gsus2/E
Gsus2/D
Gsus2/C
o - pen up your morn - ing light and say a lit - tle prayer for I. You know that
Gsus2/F
Gsus2/E
Gsus2/D
Gsus2/C
if we are to stay a - live, then see the peace in ev - 'ry eye.
G(add2)
D(add4)/F♯
Em11
7fr
Dsus
I don't want to wait for our lives to be o - ver. I want

C6
G(add9)/B
Dsus/A
Dsus
G(add2)
D(add4)/F♯
to know right now, what will it be?
I don't want to wait for our lives
Em11
7fr
Dsus
C6
G(add9)/B
to be o - ver. Will it be yes, or will it be...
1
Dsus/A
Dsus
2
Dsus/A
G(add2)
sor - ry?
Du du du du du,
C6/9
1
du du du du du,
du du du du du du.

2
Gsus2/F
Gsus2/E
So o - pen up your morn - ing light and
Gsus2/D
Gsus2/C
Gsus2/F
Gsus2/E
say a lit - tle prayer for I. You know that if we are to stay a - live, then
Gsus2/D
Gsus2/C
F(add2)
see the love in ev - 'ry eye.
Repeat and Fade

I LOVE LUCY

from the Television Series

Lyric by HAROLD ADAMSON
Music by ELIOT DANIEL

Amaj7
Dm7
A♭7♯5
G13
how we love mak - ing up a - gain.
Cmaj7
Lu - cy kiss - es like
Dm7
G7♭9
Cmaj7
no one can.
She's my mis - sus and
Cmaj7/D
C+/D
D♯dim7
Em7
I'm her man;
And life is heav -

C
Am7
D7
D#dim7
- en you see 'cause
C
Dm7
G7
C
Em7
I love Lu - cy, yes, I love Lu -
A9
D9
Dm7/G
G7
- cy and Lu - cy loves
1 C
Ab7
G7
2 C
Dm7/G
C6
me.
me.

I'M POPEYE THE SAILOR MAN

Theme from the Paramount Cartoon POPEYE THE SAILOR

Words and Music by
SAMMY LERNER

A♭
F♯dim7
E♭/G
Cm
Adim7
4fr
3fr
3fr
strong to the "fin - ich" 'cause I eats me / he eats his spin - ach; I'm / he's
B♭7
E♭
3fr
Pop - eye the Sail - or Man.
I'm / He's
A♭6
B♭7
E♭
Cm
3fr
3fr
3fr
one tough Ga - zoo - kus which hates all Pa - loo - kas wot
Fm7
B♭7
E♭
3fr
ain't on the up and square.
I / He

Ab6
Bb7
Eb
biffs 'em and buffs 'em an' al - ways out -
Cm
Fm7
Bb7
roughs 'em an' none of 'em gits no -
Eb
Ab
where. If an - y - one
Fm7
F#dim7
Eb/G
Eb
dass - es to risk {my / his} "fisk" it's

E♭7
A♭
4fr
"Boff" an' it's "Wham," un - 'er - stan'?
C7
Fm
Fm7
B♭7
So, keep "Good Be - hav - or," that's
E♭
3fr
Cm
3fr
Fm
Fm7
your one life - sav - er with Pop - eye the
B♭7
E♭
3fr
Sail - or Man.
I'm
He's

E♭
3fr
B♭7
E♭
3fr
Pop - eye the Sail - or Man,
E♭7
A♭
4fr
E♭
3fr
I'm
he's
Pop - eye the Sail - or Man.
A♭
4fr
F♯dim7
E♭/G
3fr
I'm
He's
strong to the "fin - ich" 'cause
I eats me
he eats his
Cm
3fr
Adim7
B♭7
E♭
3fr
spin - ach;
I'm
he's
Pop - eye the Sail - or Man.

I'M SO GLAD WE HAD THIS TIME TOGETHER

Carol Burnett's Theme from THE CAROL BURNETT SHOW

By JOE HAMILTON

Dm7
A♭9♭5
G9sus
3 fr
Cmaj7
Emaj7
E♭6/9
Dm7
A♭9♭5
G9sus
3 fr
time you put a - side for dream-in', and a time for things you have to do.
Cmaj7
Dm7
G7
Em9
A7♯5(♭9)
But the time I like the best is an - y eve - ning I can
Dm7
G13
2 fr
C6
Bm7
2 fr
E7
spend a mo-ment here with you. When the time comes and I'm feel - ing
Amaj7
F♯m7
F7
Bm7/E
E9
Amaj7
F♯m7
C♯m7
4 fr
F♯7
lone - ly, when I'm feel - in' oh so blue, I just sit back and think of you

Bmaj7
G♯m7
4 fr
C♯m11
4 fr
F♯9
3 fr
F♯m7
F7
Emaj7
E♭6/9
on - ly and the hap - pi - ness still comes_ through. I'm so
Dm7
A♭7♭5
G9sus
3 fr
Cmaj7
Emaj7
E♭6/9
Dm7
A♭7♭5
G9sus
3 fr
glad we had this time to - geth - er 'cause it makes me feel that I be - long.
Cmaj7
Dm7
G7
Em11
7 fr
A7♯5(♭9)
Seems we just get start - ed and be-fore you know it, guess it's
Dm7
G13
2 fr
C6
F9
C6/E
E♭dim7
Dm7
D♭maj7
Cmaj9
time for me to say, "So long."

JEANNIE

Theme from I DREAM OF JEANNIE

By HUGH MONTENEGRO
and BUDDY KAYE

G9
G+
C
C♯dim7
3 fr
- to! The rain goes. She blinks. Up comes the rain - bows!
Dm
Dm7
G9
G+
C
Cars stop, e - ven the train goes slow when
C7
Fm7
B♭7
she goes by! She paints sun - shine on ev - 'ry
E♭maj7
Cm7
Fm
raf - ter, sprin - kles the air with laugh - ter. We're close

Dm7♭5
G7sus
G7
N.C.
as a quar - ter af - ter three. There's no one like
Dm
Dm7
G7
G+
3 fr
C
Jean - nie. I'll in - tro-duce her to you, but
C♯dim7
Dm
Dm7
G7
G+
3 fr
it's no use, sir, 'cause my Jean - nie's in love with
1
C
me!
2
C
Gm7/D
3 fr
D♭7♭5
C
me!

IT'S HOWDY DOODY TIME

Theme from THE HOWDY DOODY SHOW

Words and Music by
EDWARD GEORGE KEAN

C
Doo - dy time, it's How - dy Doo - dy time. Bob Smith and
G7
C
How - dy Doo say how - dy doo to you. Let's give a
rous - ing cheer 'cause How - dy Doo - dy's here. It's time to
G7
C6
start the show, so, kids, let's go!

THE LIBERTY BELL

from MONTY PYTHON'S FLYING CIRCUS

By JOHN PHILIP SOUSA

Moderate tempo, in 2

F Bb F Bb Gm

f

C7 F C7

mf

F

G7
C/G
G7
C
G7
C
G7
1 C
2 C
C7/E
F
f
B♭
C7
F
C7

F
Dm7(♭5)
C/G
G7
C
B♭
A
A7/C♯
Dm
Gm/B♭
A
Gm/B♭
F/C
1
C7
F
2
F
8va basso

LOVE AMERICAN STYLE

Theme from the Paramount Television Series LOVE AMERICAN STYLE

Words and Music by ARNOLD MARGOLIN
and CHARLES FOX

Gm7/C
C7sus
Fmaj7
you.
me.
And on a star -
We pledge our love
G/F
- span - gled night,
'neath the same
my love
old moon
Gm7♭5/F
Gm7♭5/C
8fr
Fmaj7
you can rest your head on my shoul - der.
But it shines red and white and blue now.
While by the dawn's ear - ly light
And in this land of hopes and dreams,

G/F
Gm7♭5/F
my love
my love
I will de - fend
all that I hope
Gm7♭5/C
8fr
1
F
your right to try.
for 'tis of thee.
2
F
B♭
Love A -
Love A -
Am7
Gm7
3fr
C7sus
F
Repeat and Fade
mer - i - can style,
fre - er than the land of the blue.
mer - i - can style,
tru - er than the red, white and blue.

LINUS AND LUCY

By VINCE GUARALDI

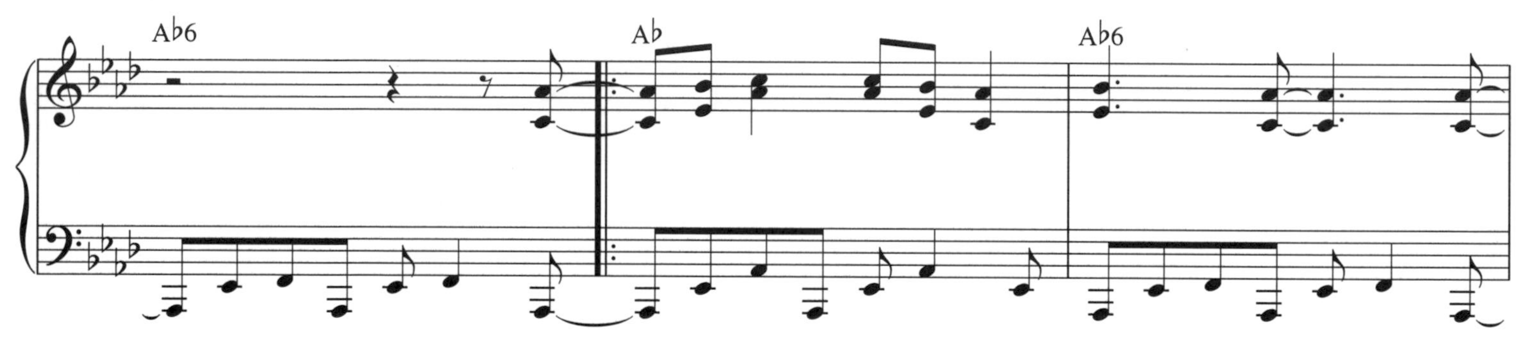

1
2
Ab
Ab6
Ab6
Db
Eb
Db
Eb
Db
Eb
Ab
Ab6
Ab
Ab6
Ab
Ab6

Ab
Ab6
Cb
Cb6
Ab
Ab6
Cb
Cb6
Ab
Ab6
N.C.
Eb7
Db

C7
D♭7
E♭9

E♭7
E♭

D♭
3
C7

D♭7
D7
E♭7

A♭
A♭6
A♭

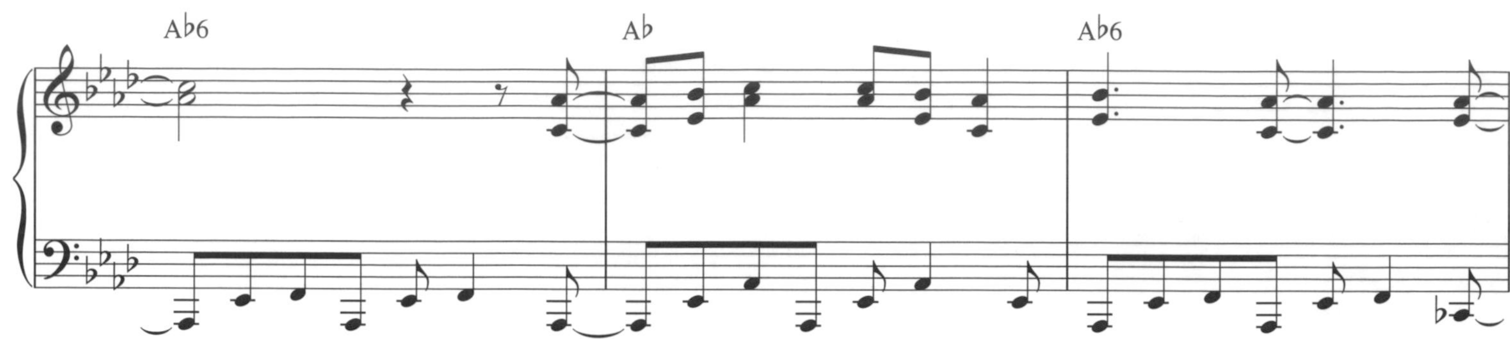
A♭6
A♭
A♭6

C♭
C♭6
A♭

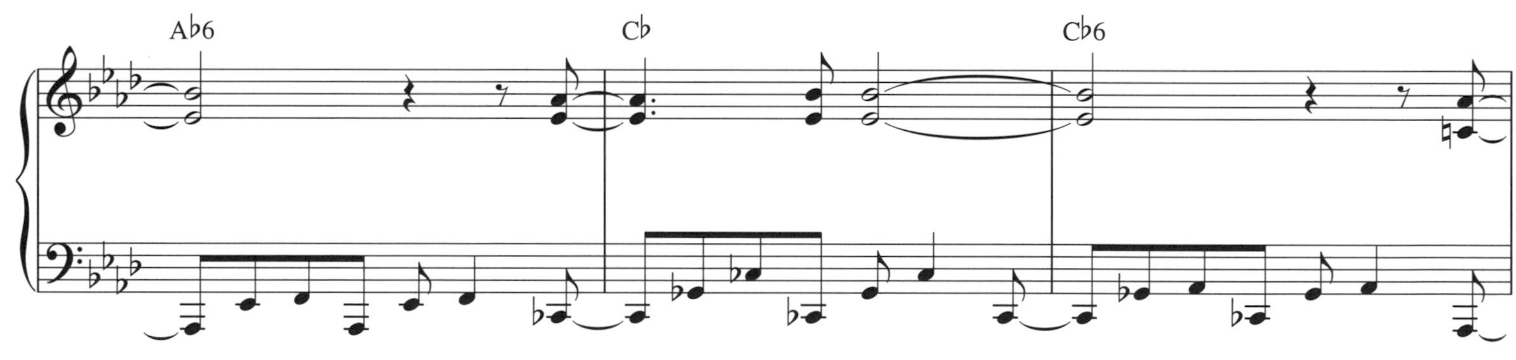
A♭6
C♭
C♭6

Swing feel
A♭
A♭6
N.C.
E♭7

D♭7

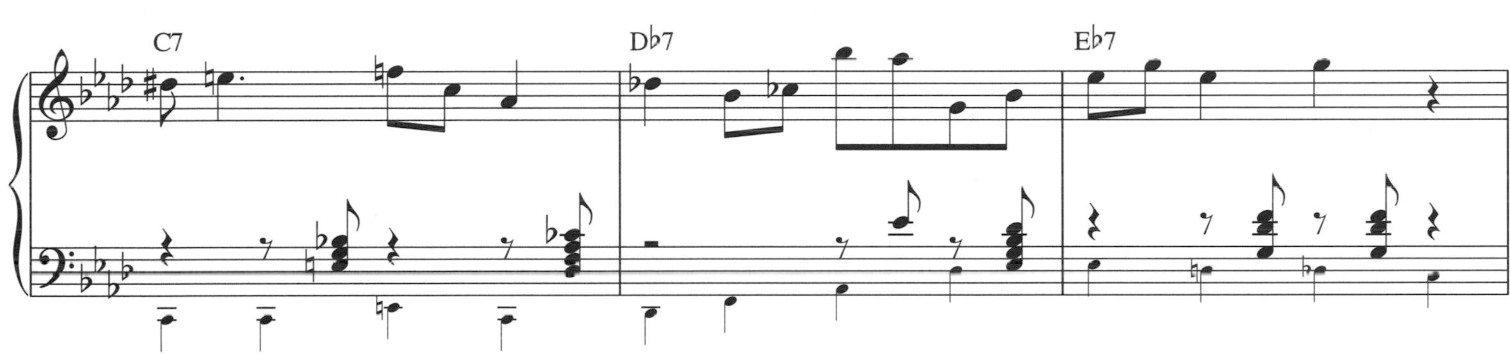
C7
D♭7
E♭7

E7
E♭7

D♭7

C7
D♭7
D7
Original Tempo (♩♪ = ♩♪)
E♭7
A♭
A♭6
A♭
A♭6
A♭
A♭6
C♭
C♭6
A♭
A♭6
C♭

C♭6
A♭
A♭6
A♭
A♭6
A♭
A♭6
A♭
A♭6
A♭
A♭6
A♭
A♭6

THE LITTLE HOUSE
(On the Prairie)
Theme from the TV Series

Music by DAVID ROSE

E♭6/9
Dm(add9)
D9
G
Am/G
G
G9
C
Am7
Am6
G/B
Fmaj7/G
G7
C6/G
C/G
D
D/C
G/B
G7
C
D7
G(add9)
F6/9
E♭6
D9sus
G(add9)
rit.

LOVE BOAT THEME

from the Television Series

Words and Music by CHARLES FOX
and PAUL WILLIAMS

Cm7
3fr
Come a - board. We're ex -
Cm7/F
F7
B♭
pect - ing you. And love,
Gm7
3fr
3
life's sweet - est re - ward. Let it
E♭maj7
3fr
Cm7
3fr
float. It floats back to you.

Cm7/F
Fm7/B♭
B♭7
The love boat soon will be
E♭maj7
3fr
E♭m7/A♭
11fr
mak - ing an - oth - er run. The love boat
A♭7
4fr
D♭maj7
C7sus
C7
prom - is - es some - thing for ev - 'ry - one. Set a
Fm
Fm(maj7)
Fm7/B♭
B♭7
E♭maj7
3fr
course for ad - ven - ture, your mind on a new ro - mance.

Cm7
3fr
Bmaj7
B♭
3
And love
f
Gm7
3fr
won't hurt an - y - more.
Cm7
3fr
It's an o - pen smile
Cm/F
5fr
on a friend - ly shore.

F7
Eb/F
Bb
It's
love.
Ab/Bb
Eb/F
Bb
It's
love.
3
Ab/Bb
Eb/F
Bb
Ab/Bb
Eb/F
Bb

MAKING OUR DREAMS COME TRUE

Theme from the Paramount Television Series LAVERNE AND SHIRLEY

Words by NORMAN GIMBEL
Music by CHARLES FOX

F/C
Dm
C/E
We're gon - na make our dreams come true,
C
B♭
C
F
A7
do - in' it our way. Noth - ing's gon - na turn us back now,
Dm
B♭
straight a - head and on the track now.
F/C
Dm
C/E
We're gon - na make our dreams come true,

A7
Dm7
G
do - in' it our way. There is noth - ing we won't try;
Cmaj7
C
nev - er heard the word im - pos si - ble.
B♭maj7
Gm6/B♭
F
This time there's no stop - ping us.
C
B♭
C
F
We're gon - na do it. On your mark, get set,

A7
Dm
B♭
and go now.
Got a dream and we just know now,
F/C
Dm
we're gon - na make that dream come
C/E
C7
F
true, and we'll do it our way, yes
Dm
B♭
our way.
Make all our dreams come
3

C7
F
Dm
true, and do it our way, yes our way.
B♭maj7
3
Make all our dreams come true
C7
for me and
B♭
F/A
Gm7
3fr
B♭
F/A
Gm7
3fr
F
you.

MacGYVER

Theme from the Paramount TV Series MacGYVER

Words and Music by
RANDY EDELMAN

Bright Rock

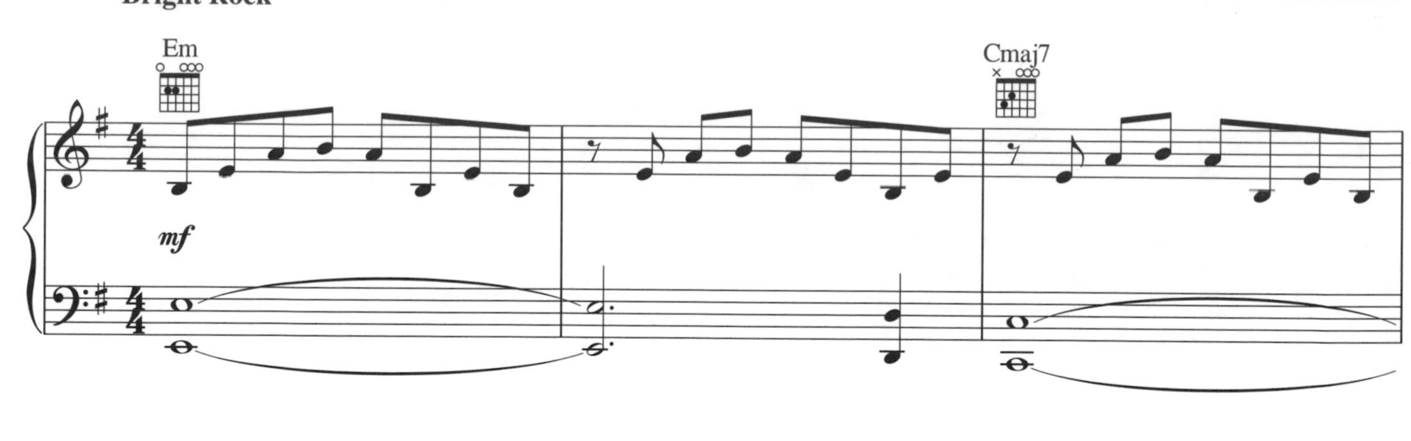

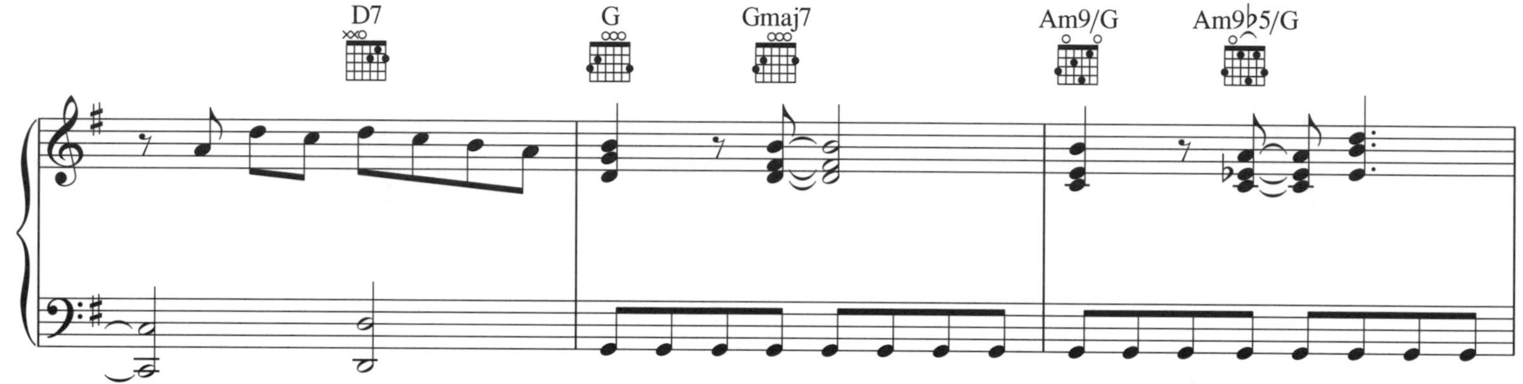

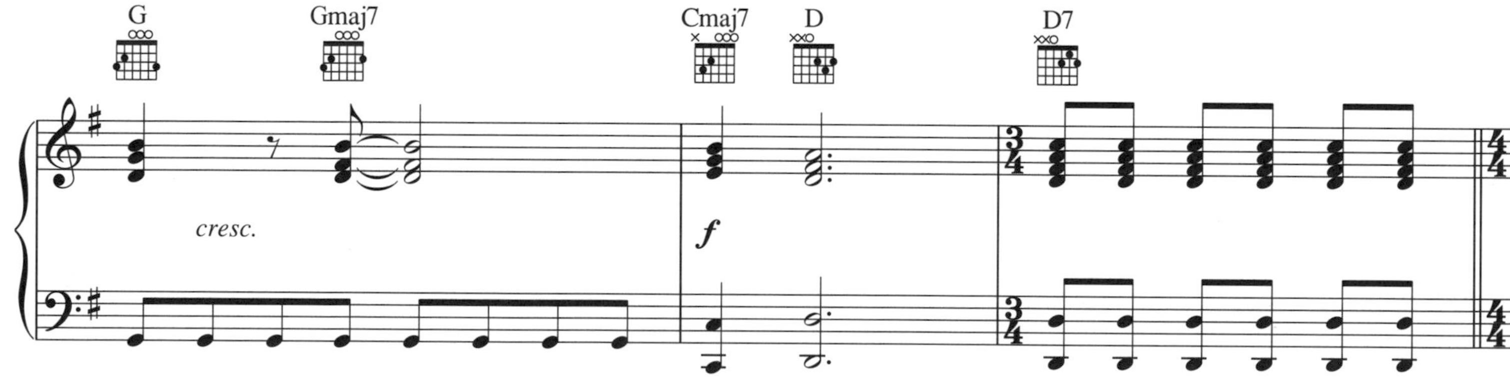

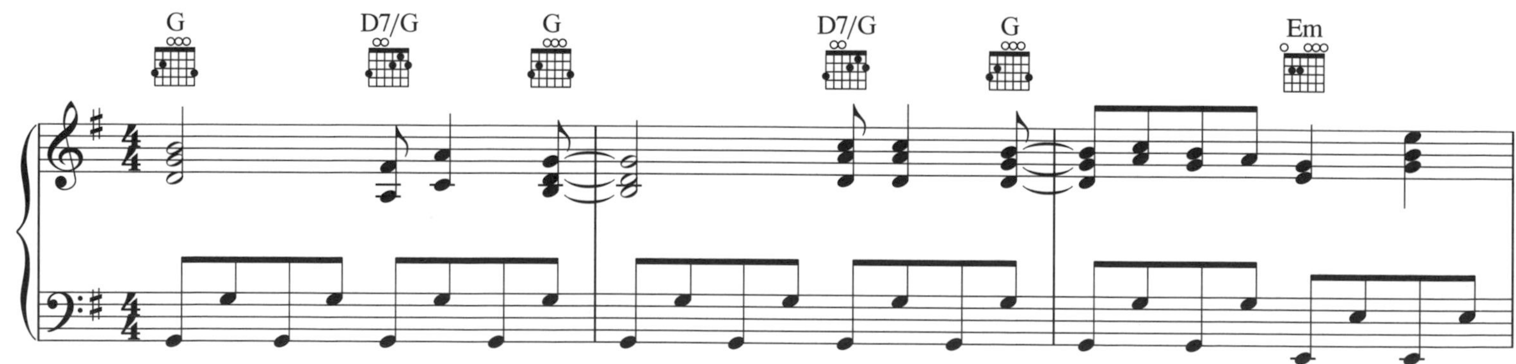

Am/C
D7
G
D7/G
G
D7/G
G
Em
Am/C
E7/B
Am
D7/F♯
G/B
C
B7
Em
B/D♯
G7/D
G7
Cmaj7
Bm7
Am7
Gmaj7/B
C
G/D
C
E♭
D
G5
E♭/G
G5
E♭/G
G5
mf
ff

MANNIX

Theme from the Paramount Television Series MANNIX

By LALO SCHIFRIN

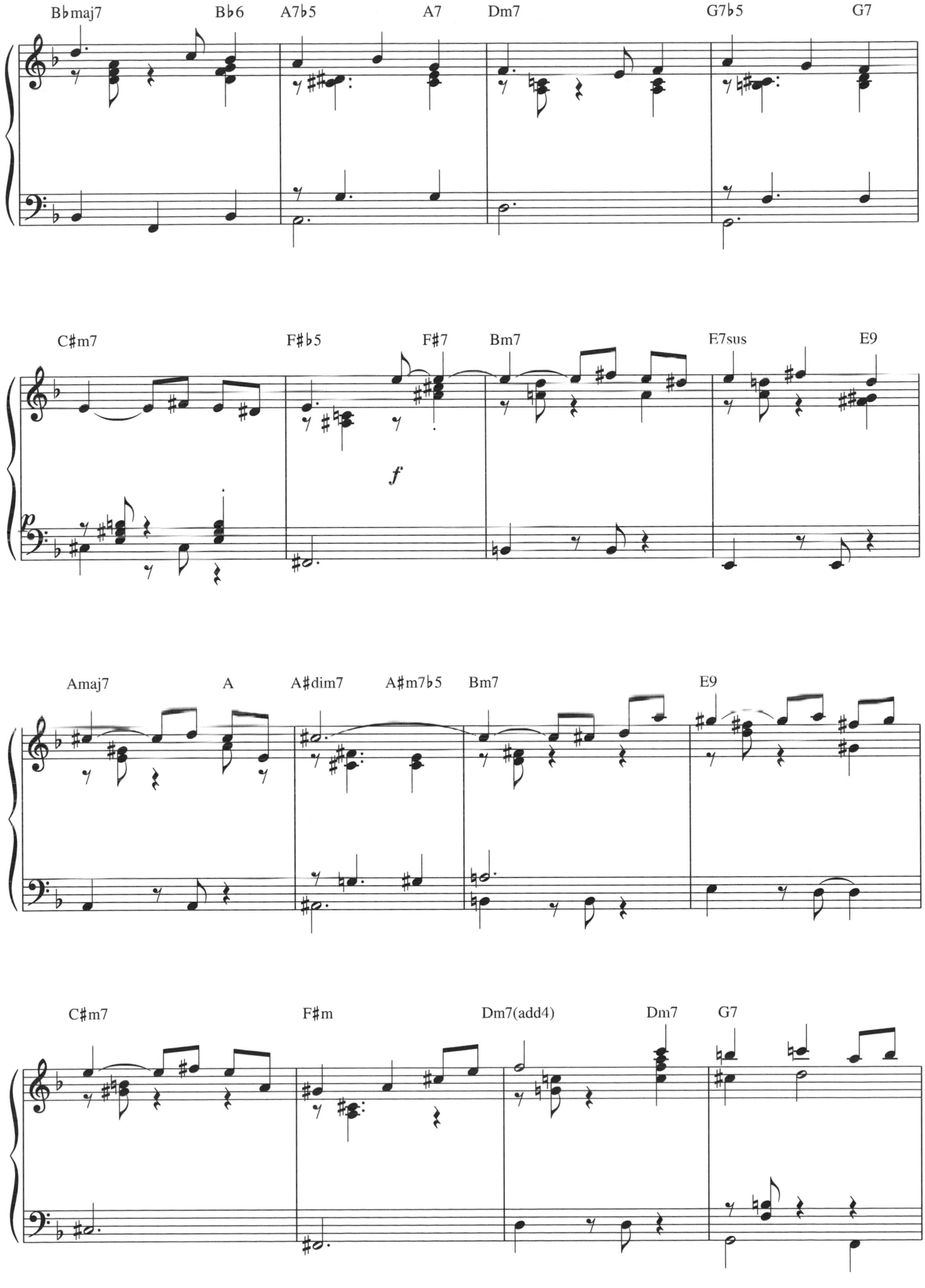

B♭maj7
B♭6
A7♭5
A7
Dm7
G7♭5
G7
C#m7
F#♭5
F#7
Bm7
E7sus
E9
p
f
Amaj7
A
A#dim7
A#m7♭5
Bm7
E9
C#m7
F#m
Dm7(add4)
Dm7
G7

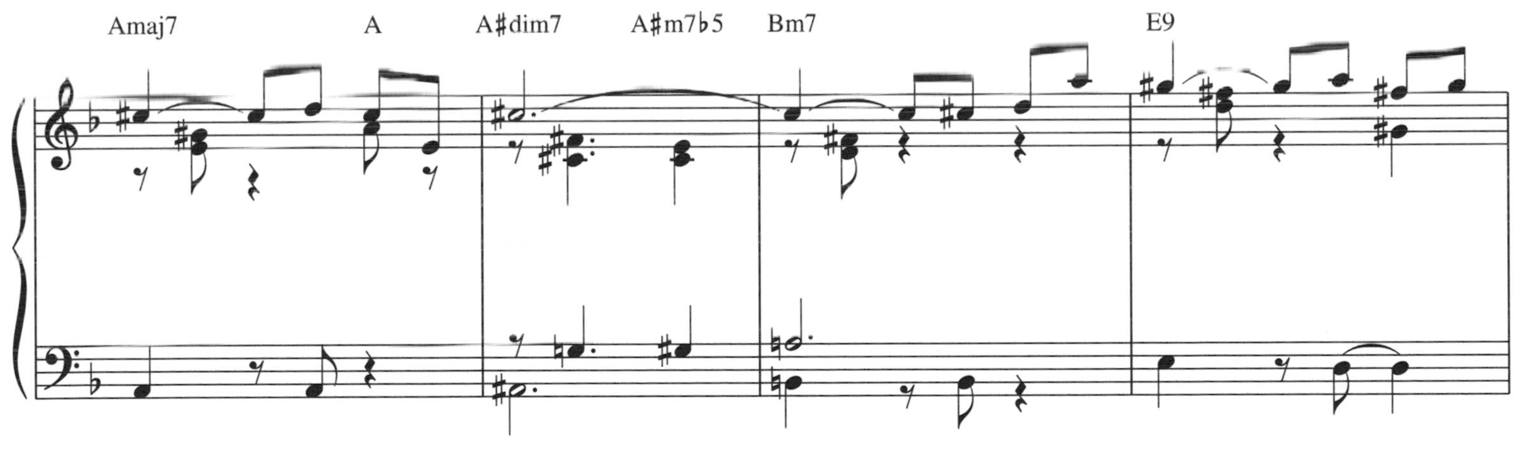

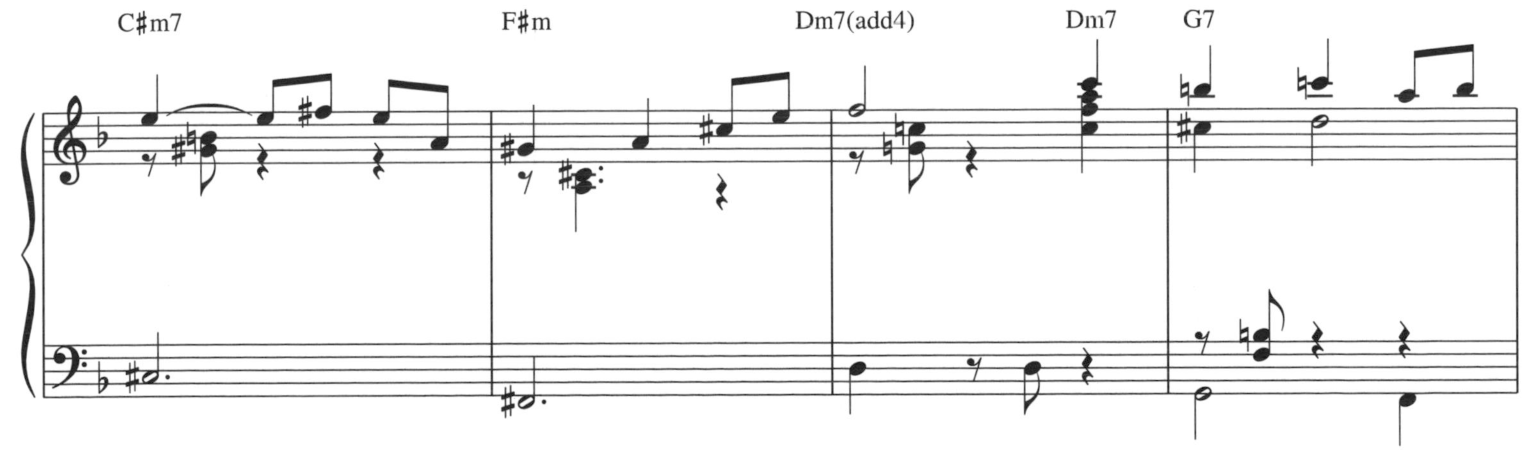

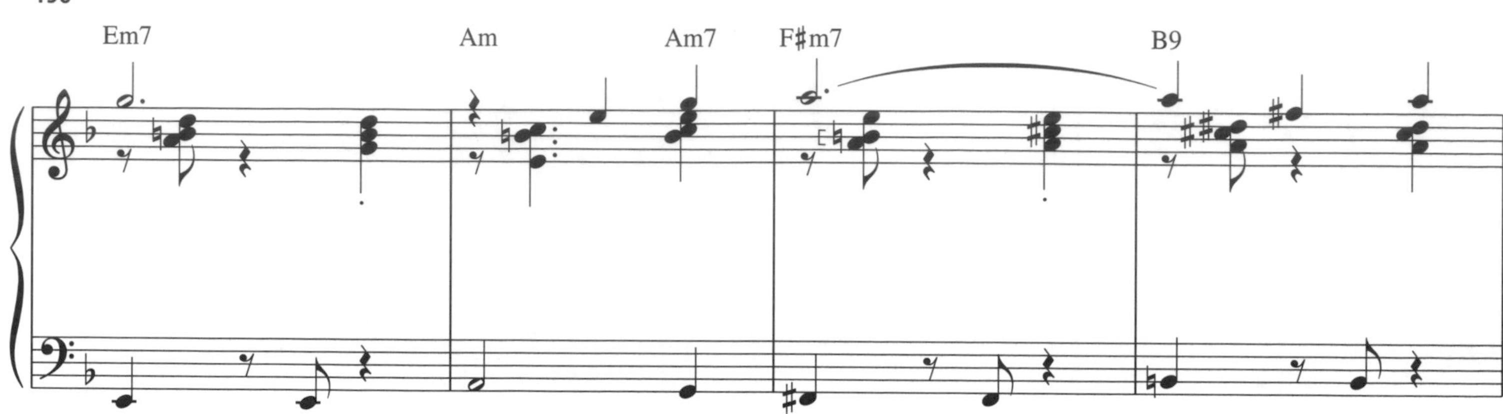
Em7
Am
Am7
F♯m7
B9

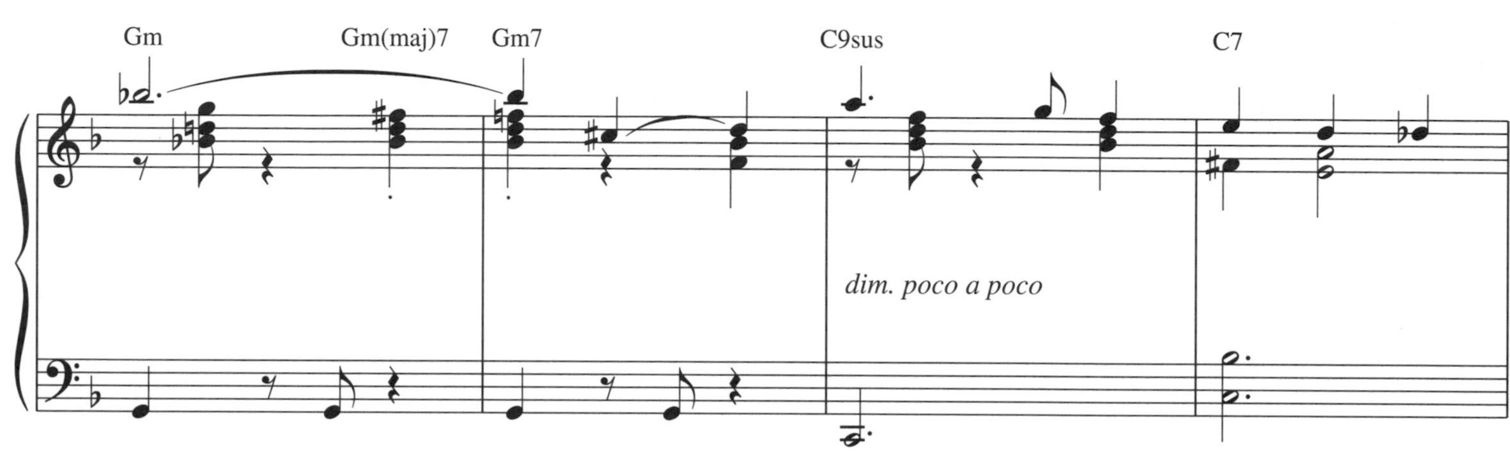
Gm
Gm(maj)7
Gm7
C9sus
C7
dim. poco a poco

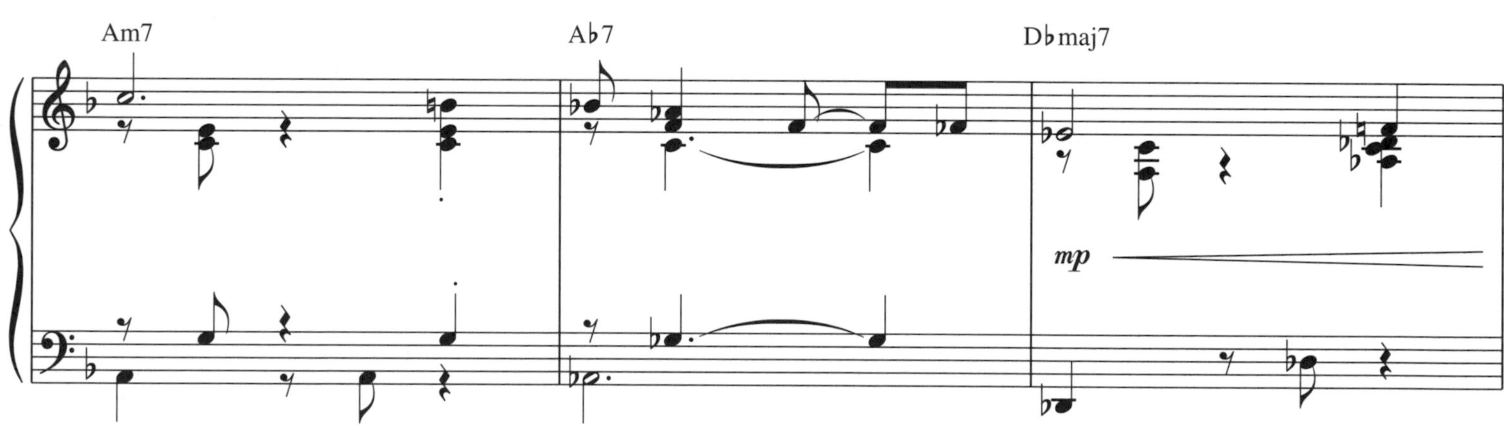
Am7
A♭7
D♭maj7
mp

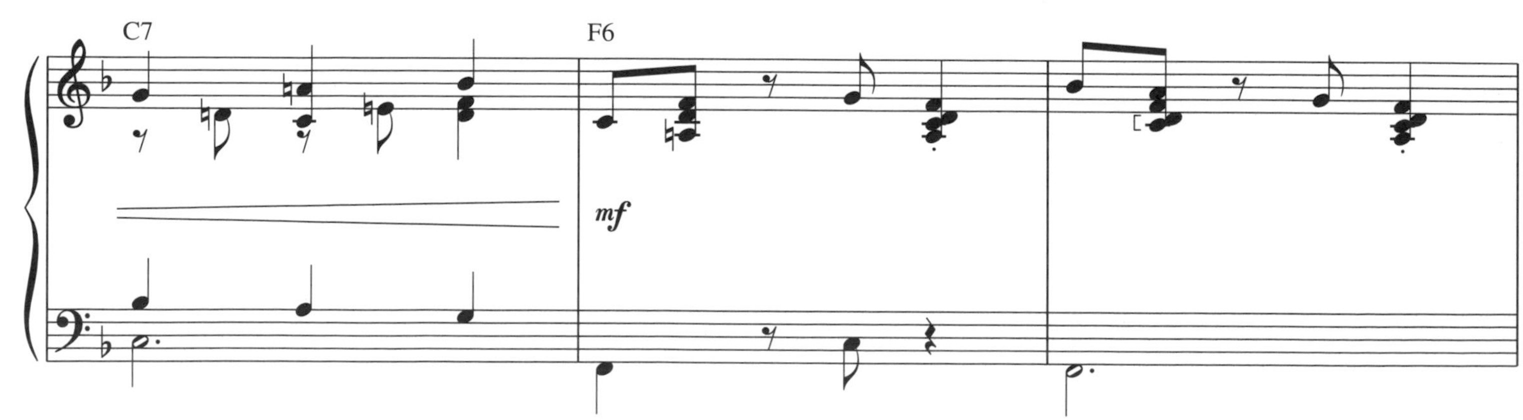
C7
F6
mf

Cm7
F6

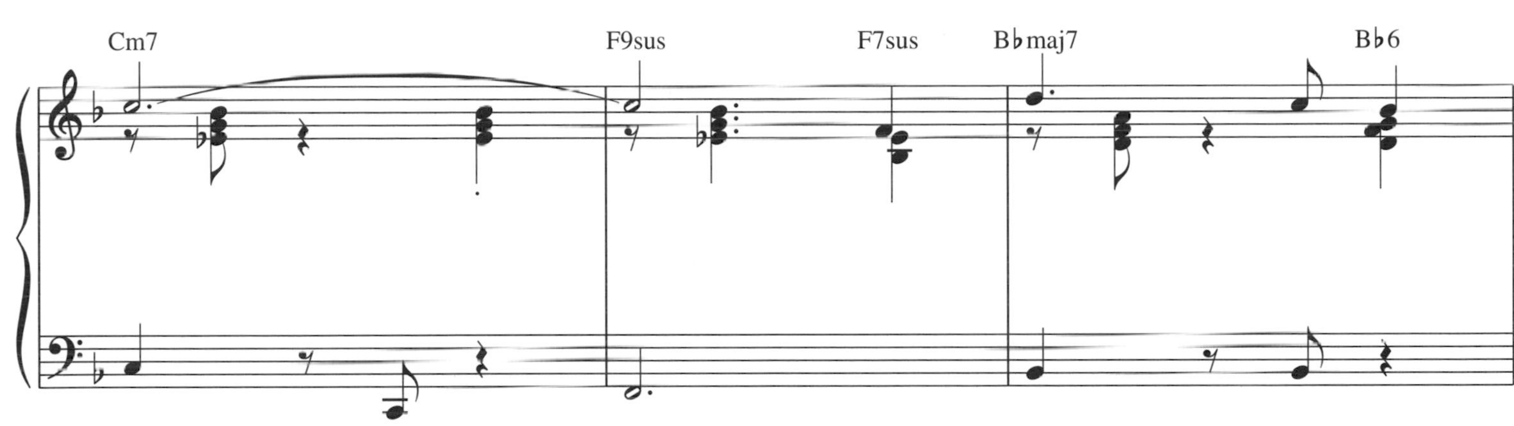
Cm7
F9sus
F7sus
B♭maj7
B♭6

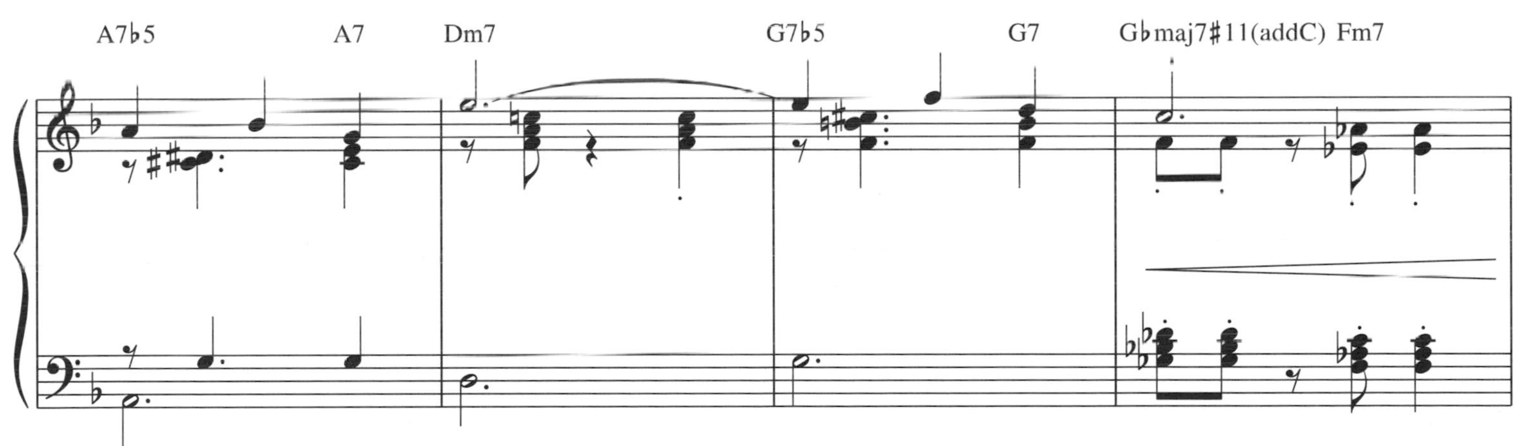
A7♭5
A7
Dm7
G7♭5
G7
G♭maj7♯11(addC)
Fm7

E♭m13
D♭6(addE♭)
C7♯5(♯9)
N.C.
ff
sfz

THE MASTERPIECE

the TV Theme from MASTERPIECE THEATRE

By J.J. MOURET
and PAUL PARNES

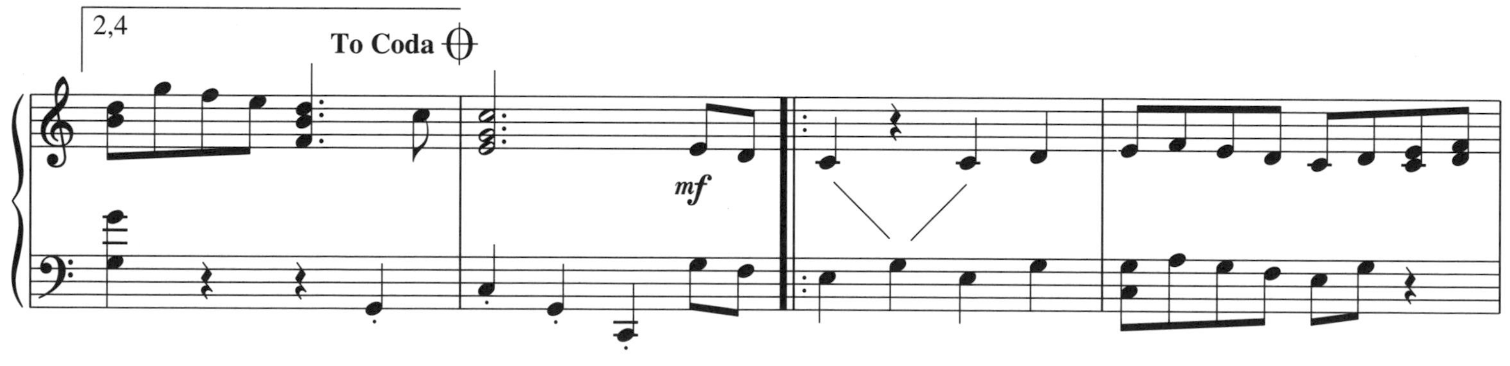

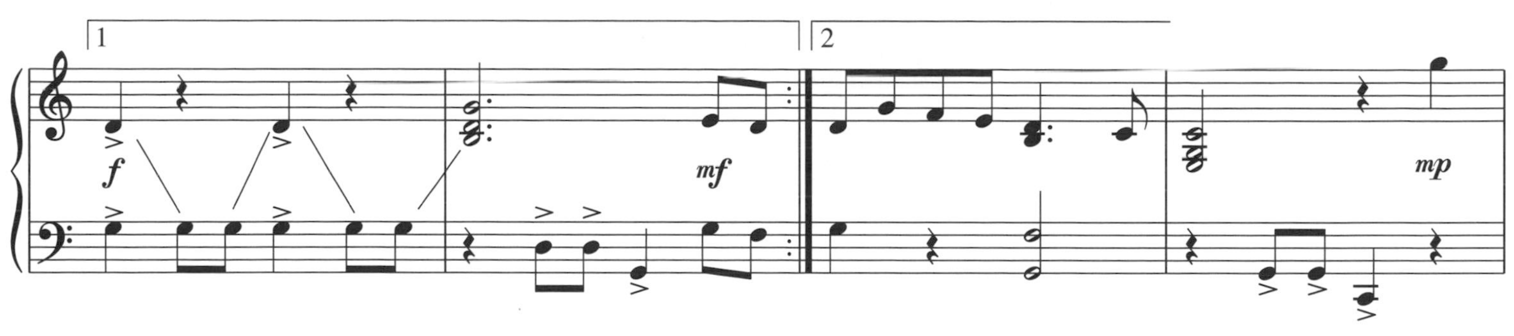
1
2
f
mf
mp

D.S. al Coda

CODA
p legato

Slower, grandly
f
broadening
ff

rit.

MISS AMERICA

from THE MISS AMERICA PAGEANT

Words and Music by
BERNIE WAYNE

C7
Gm7
C7
Cm7/F
for they may turn out to be the queen of
F7
F7♭9
B♭
B♭6
B♭maj7
B♭
fem - i - nin - i - ty. There she is Miss A -
D7
E♭
E♭6
mer - i - ca. There she is
E♭maj7
F9
B♭
Cm7
F7
B♭
G7
your i - deal. With so man - y

Cm Cm(maj7) Cm7 F13 F7♯5 B♭ D7/A
beau - ties she'll take the town by storm, _ with her all A - mer - i - can
Fm/A♭ G7♯5(♭9) E♭maj7 E♭6 E♭maj7 E♭6
face and form. _ And there she is walk - ing on
E♭m(maj7) E♭m6 E♭m(maj7) E♭m6 B♭ D7/A Gm Cm7 E♭ F7♭9
air, she is fair - est of the fair, she is Miss A - mer - i -
B♭6 Cm7 F7 B♭6
ca. ca.

MELROSE PLACE THEME

from the Television Series MELROSE PLACE

By TIM TRUMAN

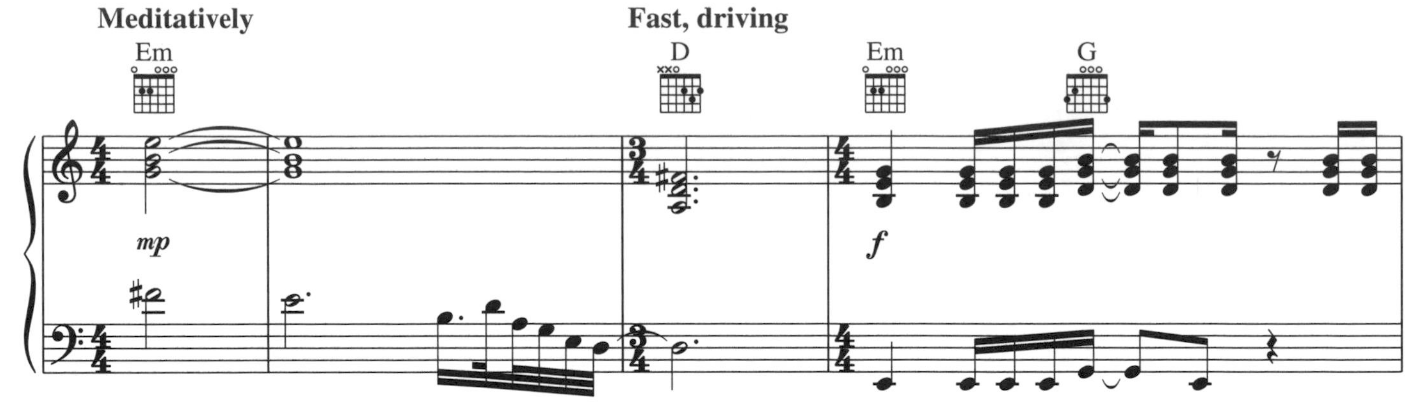

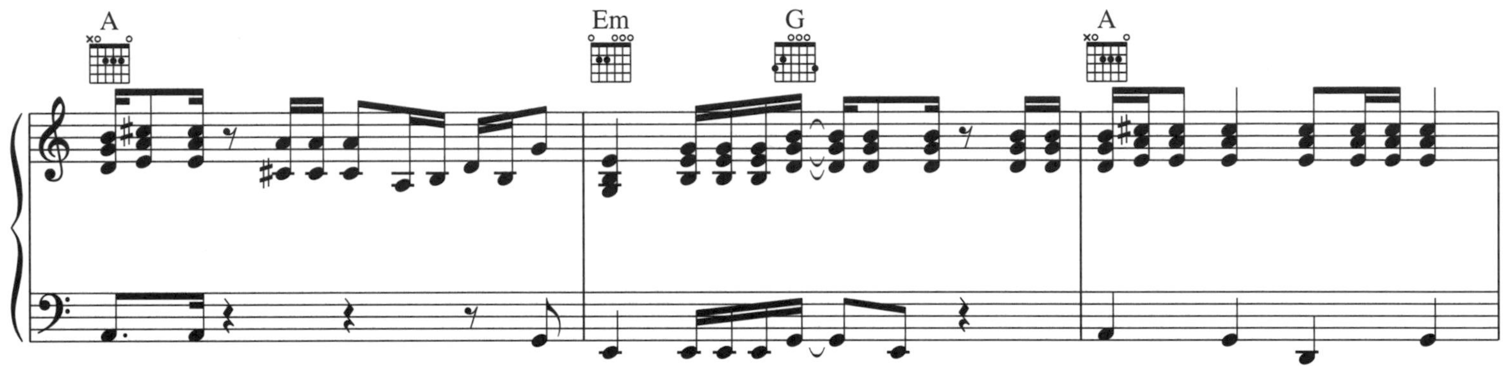

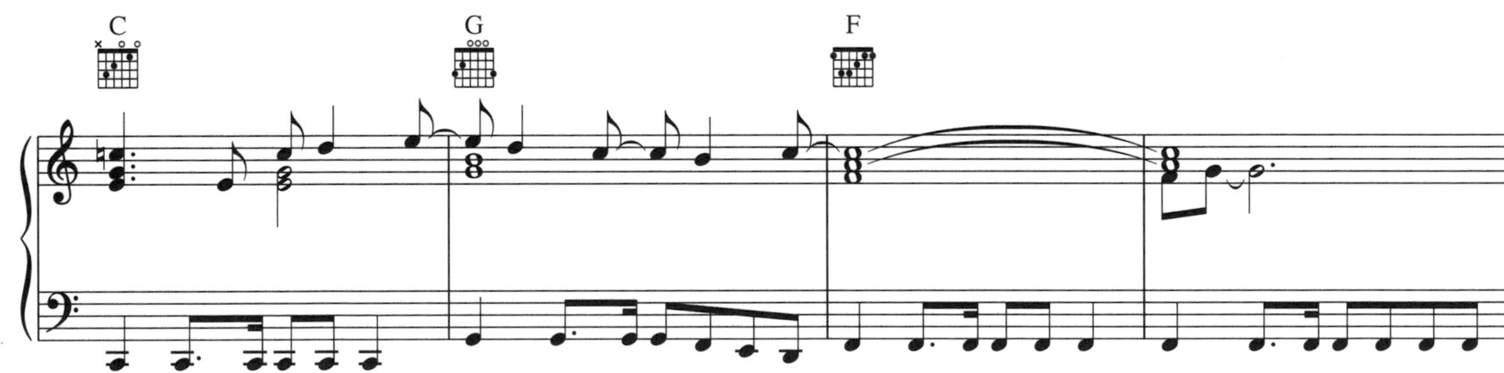

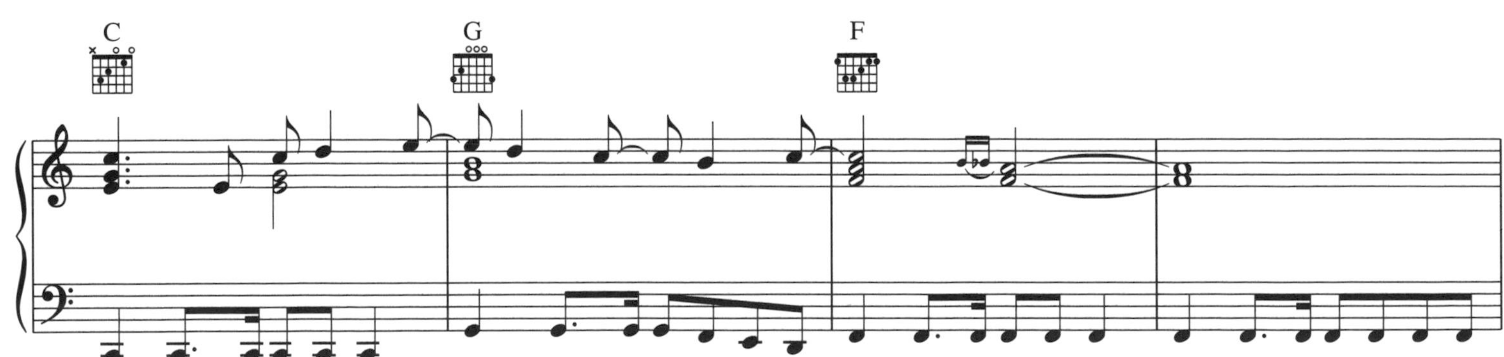

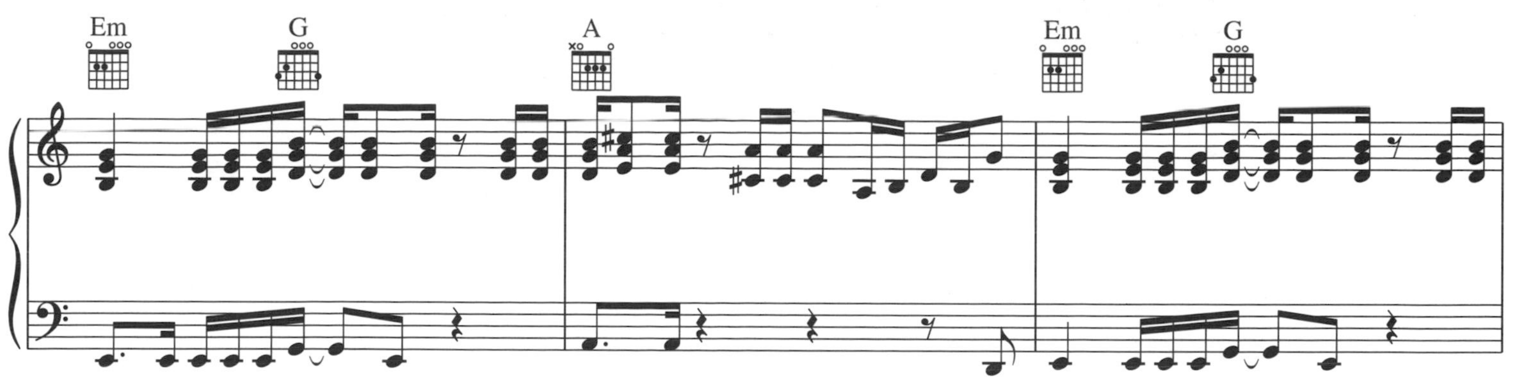
Em
G
A
Em
G

A
C
G

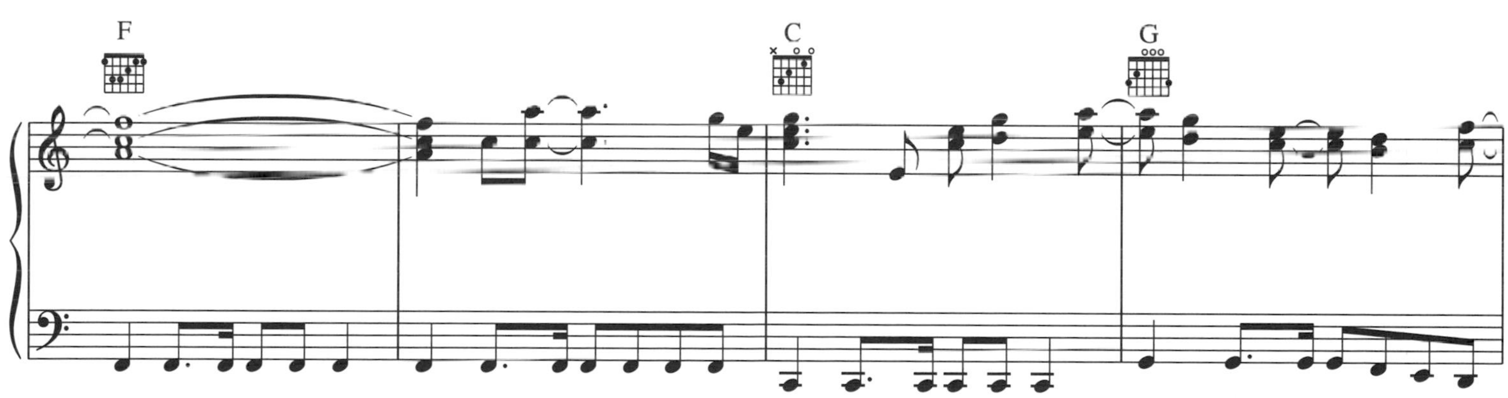
F
C
G

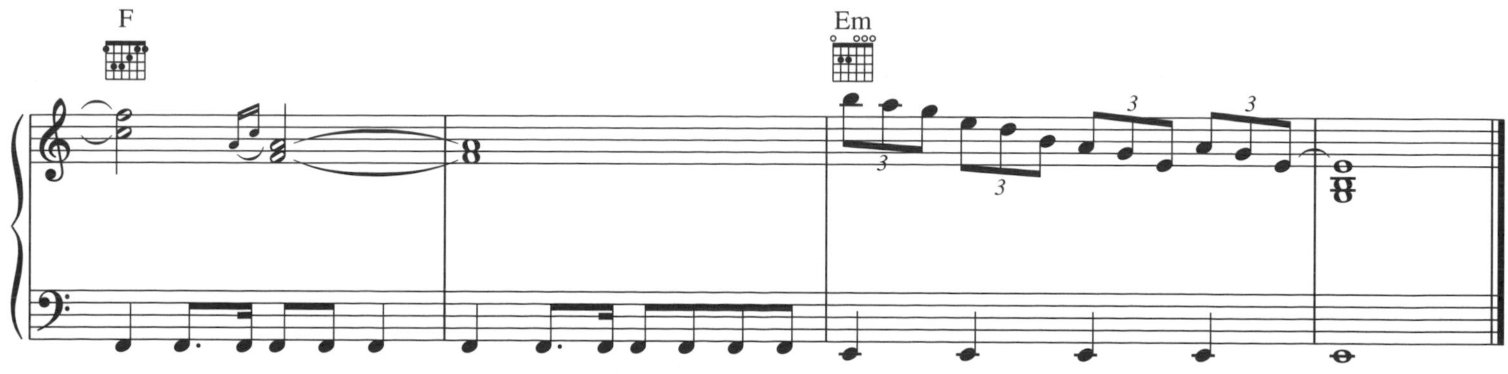
F
Em

MICKEY MOUSE MARCH

from Walt Disney's THE MICKEY MOUSE CLUB

Words and Music by
JIMMIE DODD

B♭
F
(Shout) Mick - ey Mouse!
(Shout) Don - ald Duck!
Mouse! Mick - ey Mouse! For -
G
G7
C7
(Shout) High! High! High!
ev - er let us hold our ban - ner high!
8va
cresc.
f
F
G7
C7
Come a- long and sing a song and join the jam - bor - ee!
mf
3
F
F7
B♭
B♭m
F
C7
F
M - I - C - K - E - Y M - O - U - S- E!
8va
cresc.
rit.

MISSION: IMPOSSIBLE THEME

from the Paramount Television Series MISSION: IMPOSSIBLE

By LALO SCHIFRIN

3

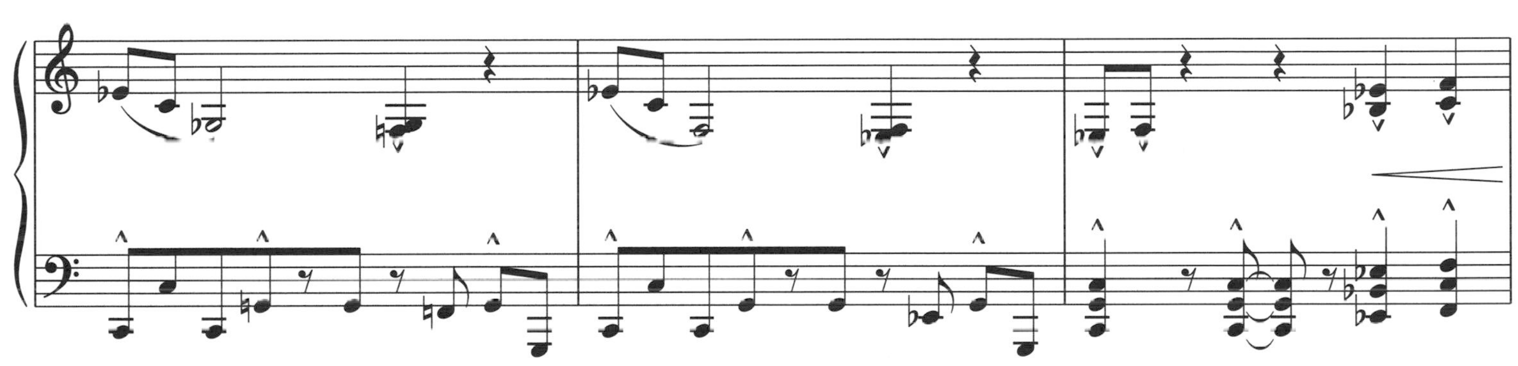

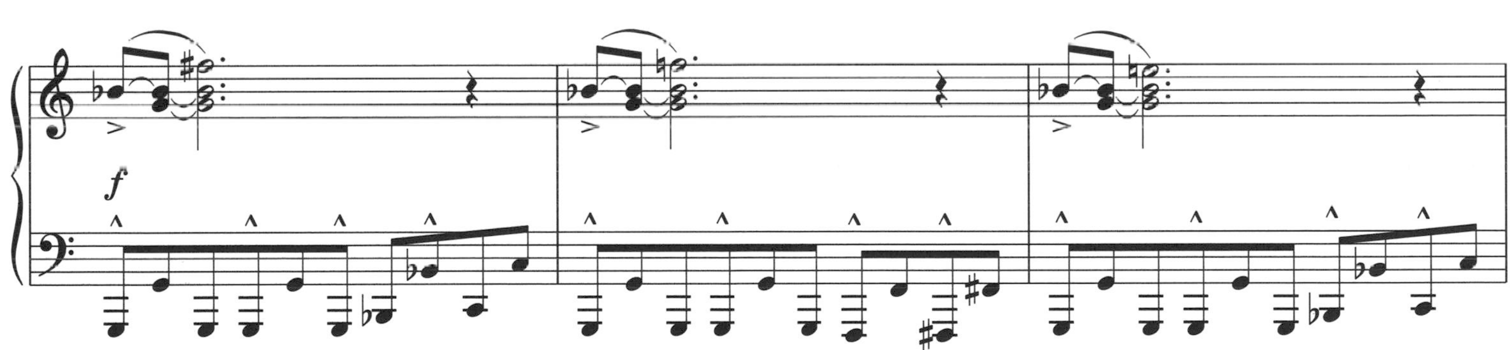
f

ff

THEME FROM "THE MONKEES"

(Hey, Hey We're The Monkees)

from the Television Series THE MONKEES

Words and Music by TOMMY BOYCE
and BOBBY HART

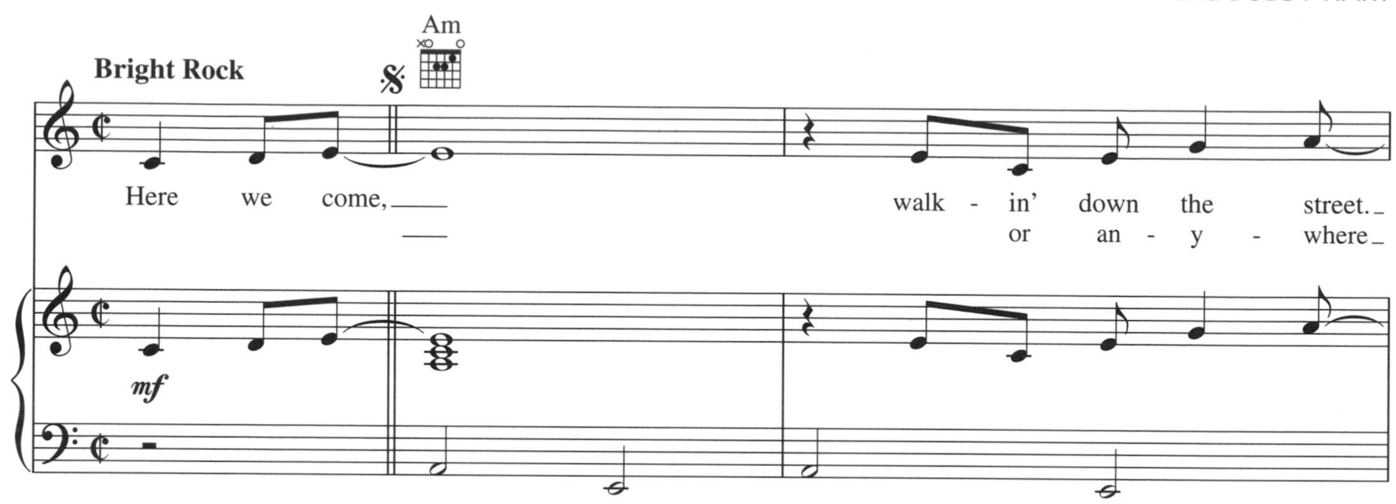

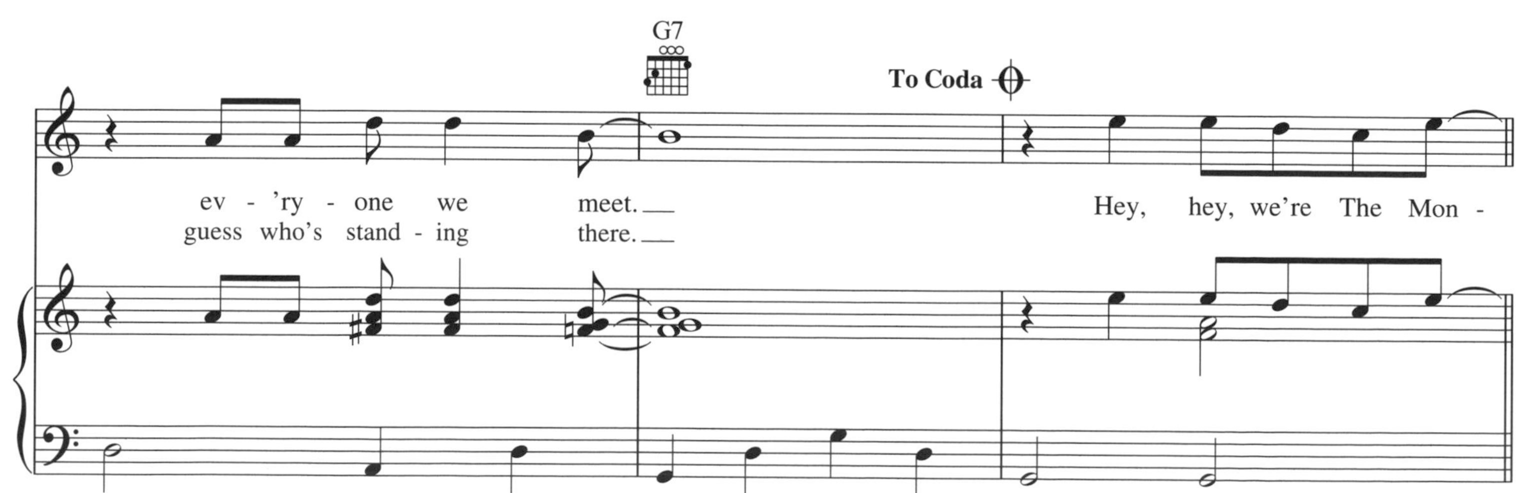

C F G C

-kees___ and peo-ple say we mon-key a-round.___ But

F G C F G

we're too bus-y sing-ing___ to put an-y-bod-y down.___

1 A5 Am

___ we go wher-ev-er we want___ to,

F

do what we like to do,___ we don't have time to get

D
G7
rest - less, there's al - ways some - thing new.
Hey, hey, we're the Mon -
2
A5
5fr
We're just try - in' to be friend -
3
D
G
A7
D
- ly, come and watch us sing and play.
G
A7
D
G
A7
We're the young gen - er - a - tion and we got some - thing to say.

B5
N.C.
D.S. al Coda
An - y - time,
CODA
G7
C
F
G
Hey, hey, we're the Mon - kees, you nev - er know where we'll be found,
C
F
G
C
so you'd bet - ter get read - y, we
F
G
A5
5fr
G7
Repeat and Fade
may be com - in' to your town.
Hey, hey, we're the Mon -

MORK AND MINDY

Theme from the Paramount Television Series MORK AND MINDY

By PERRY BOTKIN, JR.

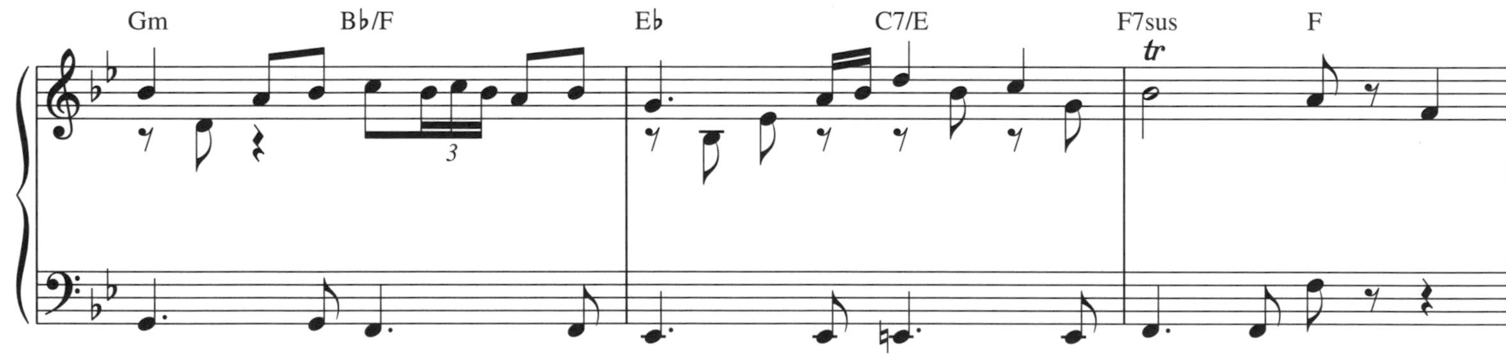

B♭A
Dm/A
Gm
B♭/F
3

E♭
C7/E
F7sus
tr
F
G(add9)

Am/G

G
Em
C
G/D
D
B♭(add9)

Cm/B♭
3
F
E♭/G
A♭7
F7/A
F7

B♭
F7/B♭

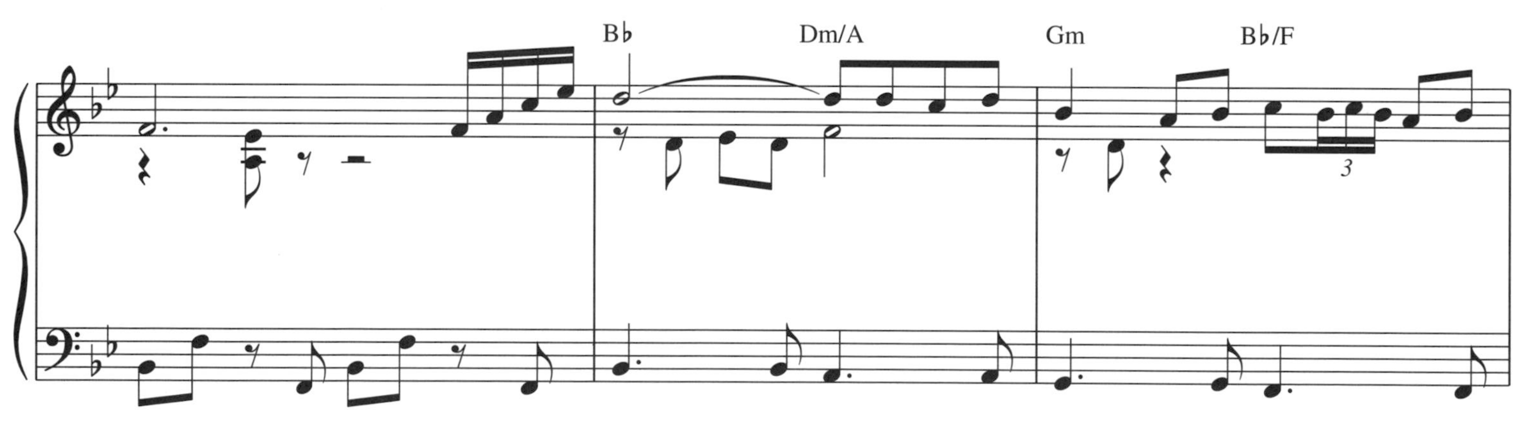
B♭
Dm/A
Gm
B♭/F
3

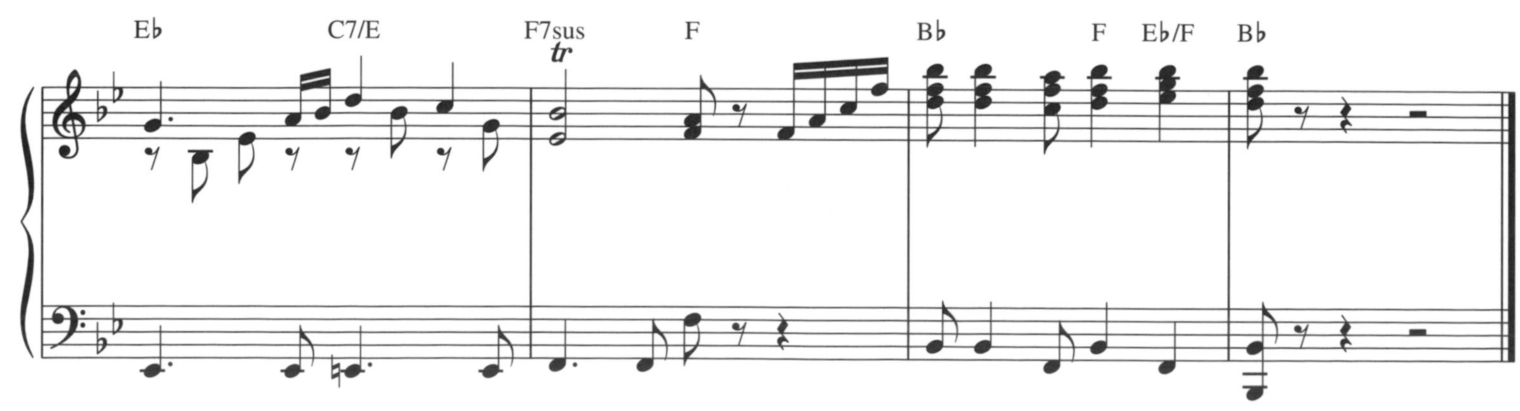
E♭
C7/E
F7sus
tr
F
B♭
F
E♭/F
B♭

THE MUPPET SHOW THEME

from the Television Series

Words and Music by JIM HENSON and SAM POTTLE

C Ebdim G7 C Ebdim G7
It's time to put on make - up. It's time to dress up right.
C C/Bb F/A Fm/Ab G13 C
It's time to raise the cur - tain on The Mup - pet Show to-night. To
F Fm C F E7 Am Am/G
in - tro - duce this rec - ord, that's what I'm here to do. So it
F E7 A7sus A7 D7sus D7 G7
real - ly makes me hap - py to in - tro- duce to you
the first, original, genuine, no money back guarantee Muppet Show Cast Album!

C
E♭dim
G7
It's time to put on make - up. It's time to dress up right.
C/B♭
F/A
Fm/A♭
C/G
F#m7-5
It's time to get things start - ed on the most sen - sa - tion - al, in - spi - ra - tion - al,
gradual cresc.
Fmaj7
F/E
Dm7
cel - e - bra - tion - al mup - pet - a - tion - al... This is what we call The
G13-9
Mup - pet Show!
ff
8va

MYSTERY

Theme from the PBS Television Series

Music by NORMAND ROGER

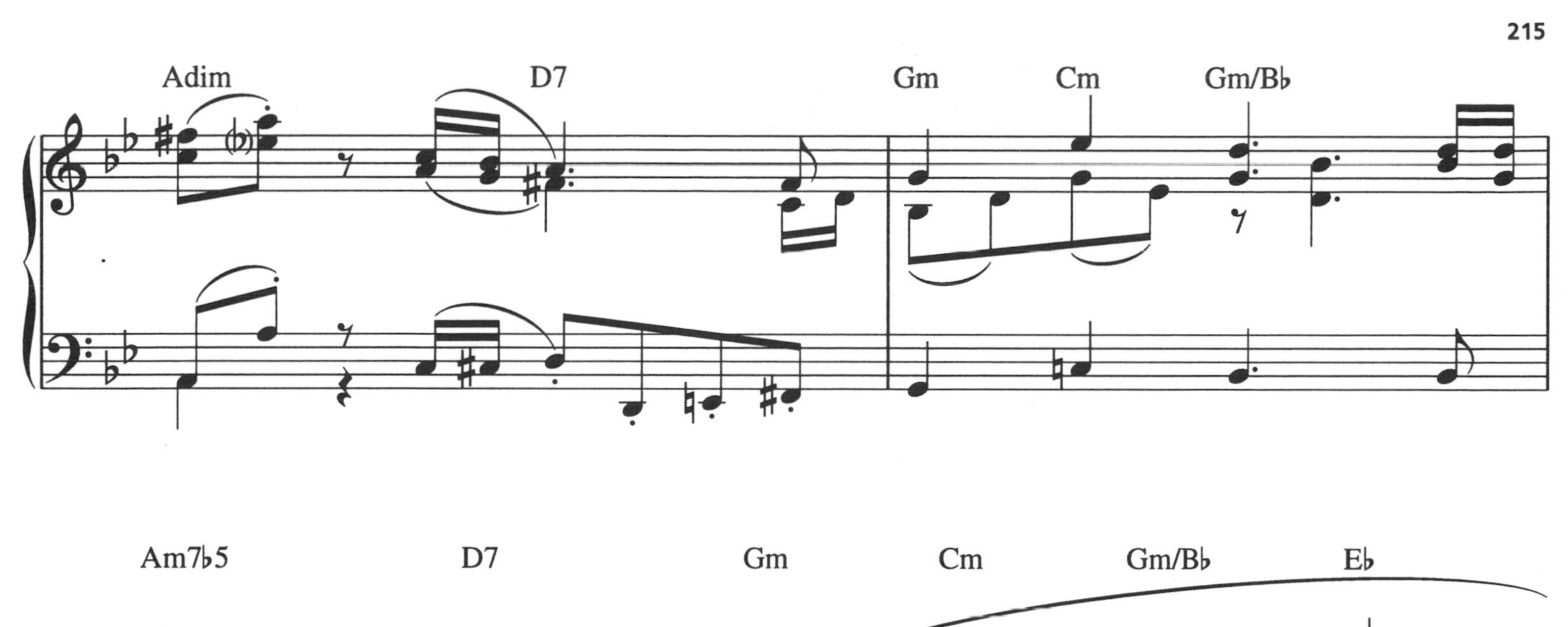
Adim
D7
Gm
Cm
Gm/B♭

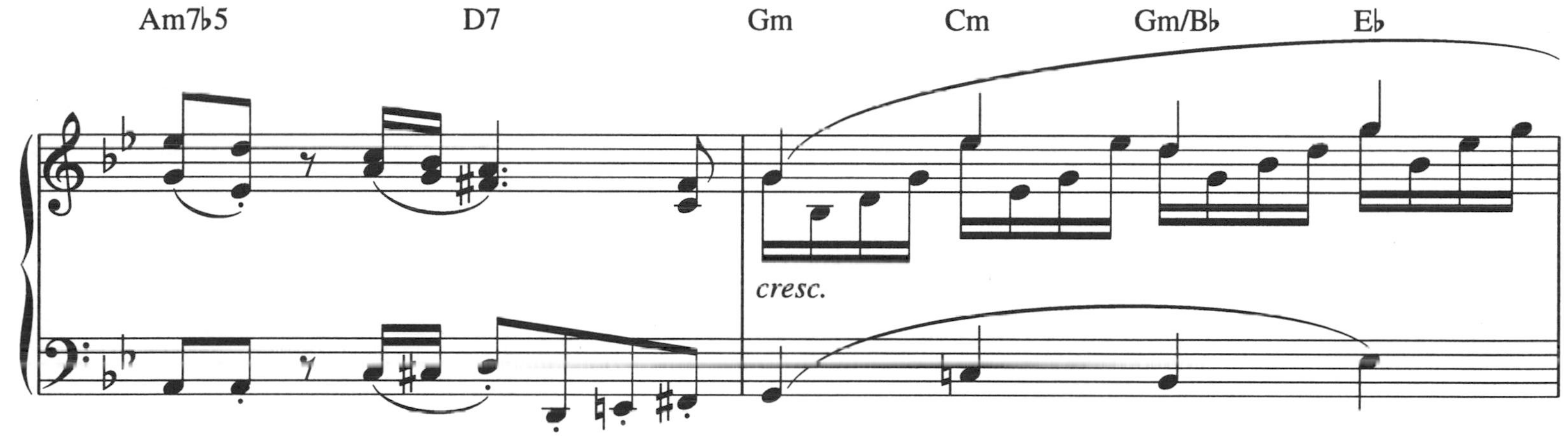
Am7♭5
D7
Gm
Cm
Gm/B♭
E♭
cresc.

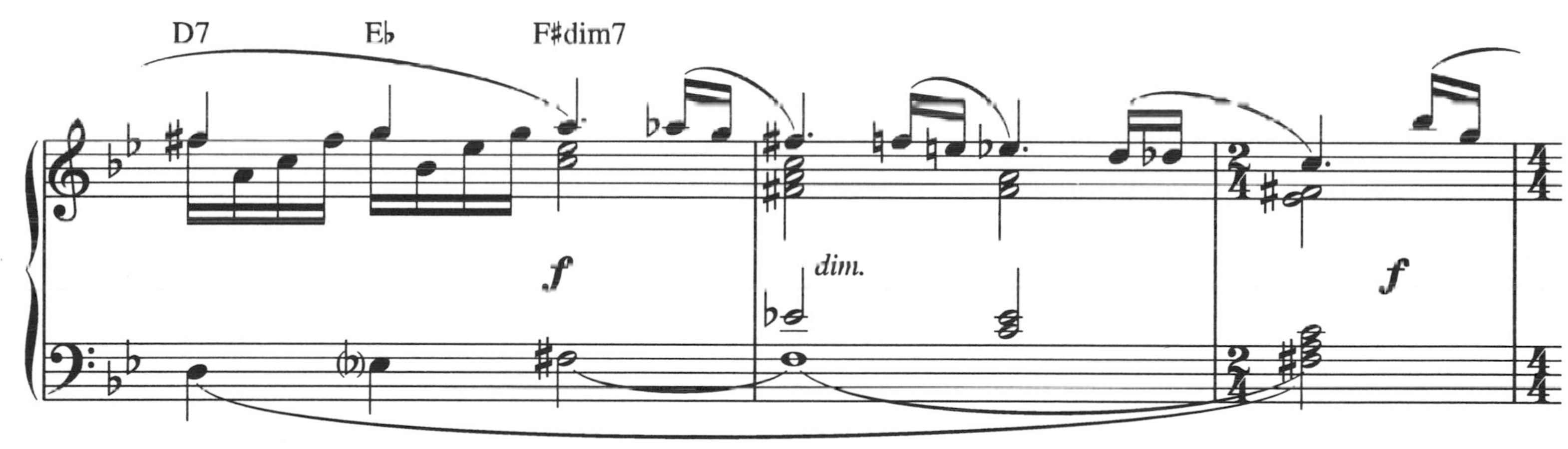
D7
E♭
F#dim7
f
dim.
f

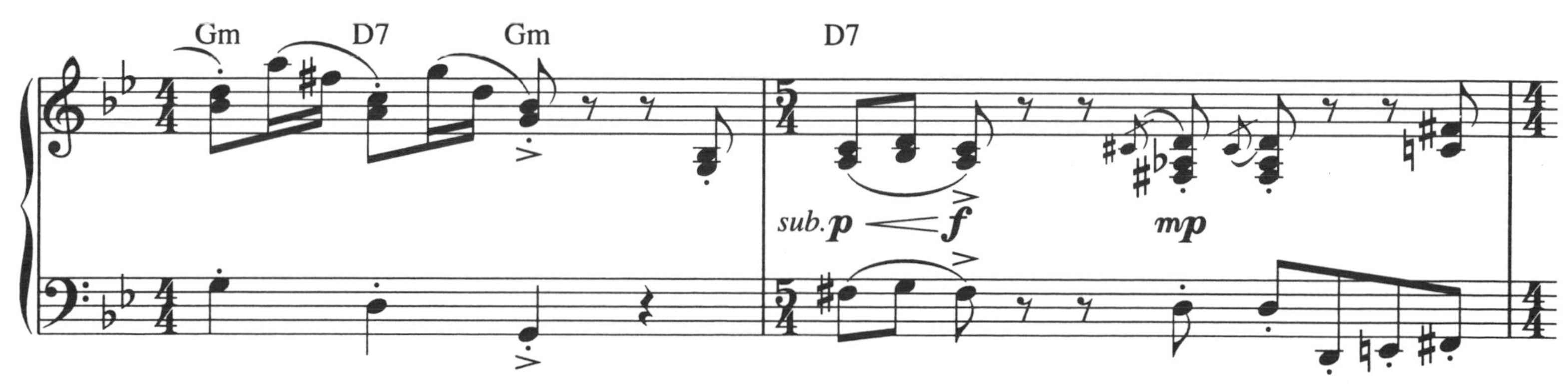
Gm
D7
Gm
D7
sub. p
f
mp

Gm Cm D7 Cm D7
Gm Cm Gm/B♭ Adim7 D7 Gm Cm Gm/B♭
Am7♭5 D7 Gm Cm Gm/B♭ E♭
cresc.
D7 Gm
dim.
mp rit.

NADIA'S THEME
from THE YOUNG AND THE RESTLESS

By BARRY DeVORZON
and PERRY BOTKIN, JR.

Gm(add2)
Gm
Cm(add2)
Cm
Cm(add2)
Cm
So
Gone, bright shin - y
drink the sum - mer
Bb(add2)
Bb
Bb(add2)
Bb
days, gone in a
wine, reach for the
Ab(add2)
Ab
Ab(add2)
Ab
Gm(add2)
Gm
young and rest - less haze.
stars while you have time.
Gm(add2)
Gm
F(add2)
F
F(add2)
F
Why did we love, then run a -
Your rest - less dreams will lead the

B♭(add2)
B♭
B♭(add2)
B♭
E♭(add2)
way? So lit - tle time, so
way, so dream your dreams and
Dm
E♭(add2)
much left to say, and now it's
live for each day while you are
1.
Gm(add2)
Gm
Gm(add2)
Gm
gone.
2.
Gm(add2)
Gm
here.
Gm(add2)
Gm
Gm(add2)
Gm

THE NAKED GUN FROM THE FILES OF POLICE SQUAD!

from the Paramount TV Series POLICE SQUAD

Music by IRA NEWBORN

1
B♭9
2
B♭9
A7♯9(♭13)
loco
Dm11
Am6
Dm11
E7♭13
E7♭9(♭13)

E7♯9(♭13)
F7♯9(♭13)
f
8vb
E♭9
F9
E9 E♭9
F9
E9 E♭9
F9
E9 E♭9
B♭9
B♭9♯11
loco

THE NANNY NAMED FRAN

from the TV series THE NANNY

Words and Music by
ANN HAMPTON CALLAWAY

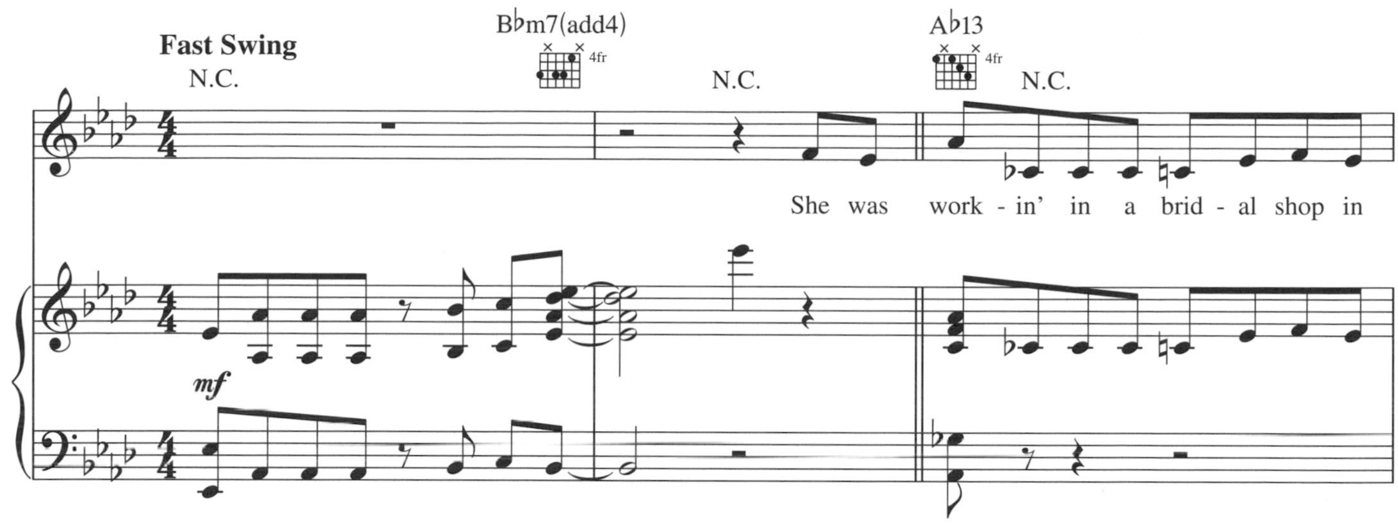

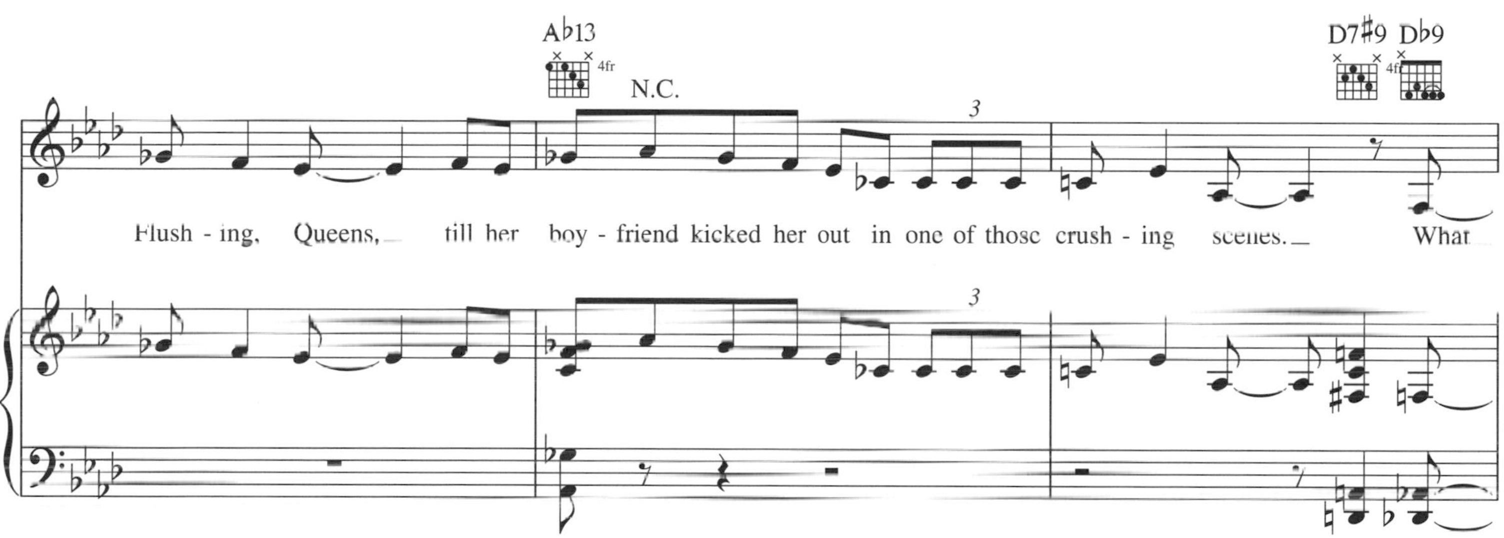

Bb7#5
Eb7#9
So, o - ver the bridge from Flush - ing to the Shef - field's door, she was
Cm7
F7#9
Bb9
Ab/C
Db
there to sell make - up, but the fa - ther saw more. She had style, she had flair, she was there,
Db/Eb
Ab6
D7#9
Db9
that's how she be - came the nan - ny. Who
Ab6
Bb7
would - 've guessed that the girl we de - scribed was just ex - act - ly what the

E♭7♯9
A♭6
3fr
N.C.
A♭6
3fr
Ddim
doc - tor pre - scribed. Now the fa - ther finds her be - guil - ing, (Watch out, C. C.) and the kids
N.C.
D♭9
are ac - tu - 'lly smil - ing. (Such joie de vivre!) She's the la - dy in red, but ev - 'ry -
C7sus
C7
Fm7
B♭9
bod - y else is wear - ing tan. The
A♭6/E♭
N.C.
flash - y girl from Flush - ing, the Nan - ny named Fran.

NATIONAL GEOGRAPHIC THEME

from the Television Series

By ELMER BERNSTEIN

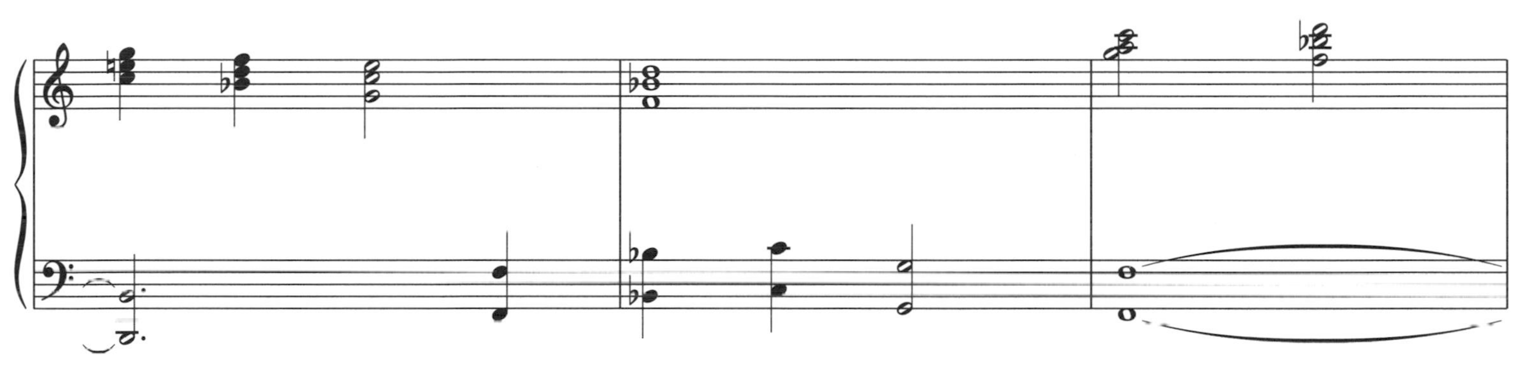

5
6
cresc.

f

THE ODD COUPLE

Theme from the Paramount Picture THE ODD COUPLE

Words by SAMMY CAHN
Music by NEAL HEFTI

F7
B7♭5
B♭maj9
B♭6
Em7
A7
As I've in - di - cat - ed they are nev - er
Dm7
G9
B♭maj7
A7♭9
6fr
Dm7
F7
quite sep - a - rat - ed, they are peas in a pod. Don't you think that it's
Em7♭5
A7
Dm7
G7
odd? Their hab - its, I con - fess,
Dm7
G7
Dm7
G7
Dm7
G7
none can guess with the cou - ple. If

Gm7
C7
Gm7
C7
one says no it's yes more or less, with the
Gm7
C7
Gm7
C7
F7
B7♭5
cou - ple. But they're laugh pro -
B♭maj9
B♭6
B♭maj9
A7♭9
vok - ing; yet they real - ly don't
Dm7
F7
B♭6
Gm7
know they're jok - ing. Don't you find when love is

C9sus
1
F
B♭9
A7♭9
6fr
blind it's kind of odd!
No
2
F
B♭m7
F(add9)/A
D7♯9
Gm7
3fr
C7
odd!
Don't you think it's odd?
Gm7
C7
Don't you think it's odd?
Gm7
C7
C6
Don't you think it's odd?
rall.

PUT YOUR DREAMS AWAY
(For Another Day)
featured in THE FRANK SINATRA SHOW

Lyric by RUTH LOWE
Music by STEPHAN WEISS and PAUL MANN

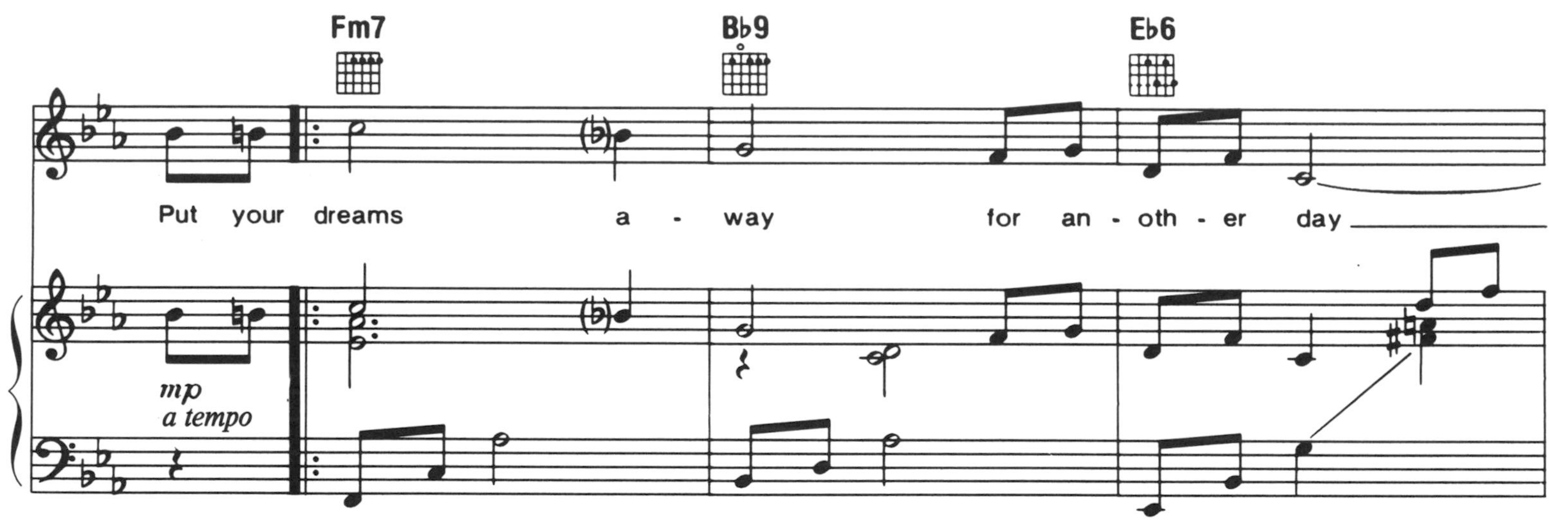

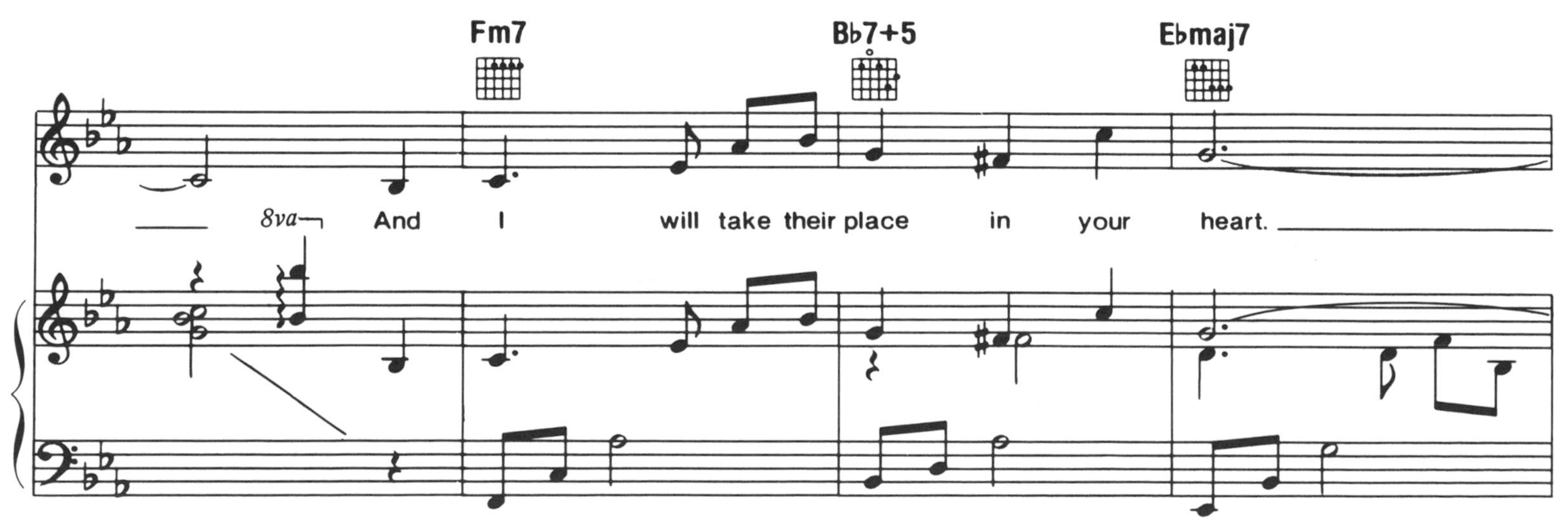

Eb6
Fm7
Bb9
Eb6
Wish-ing on a star nev-er got you far,
Eb7
G/D
D7
8va
and so it's time to make a new
Gmaj9
G7
Fm7
Ab/Bb
Bb7
start.
When your dreams at night fade be-
mf
Gm7-5
C7
Fm7-5
fore you,
then I'll have the

Db9
F9
B7+5
Bb7
right to a - dore you. Let your
8va
poco rit.
a tempo
Fm7
Bb9
Ebmaj7
Eb7
kiss con - fess this is hap - pi - ness,
C7
C7-9
Fm7
Gm7
Ab6
Fm7/Bb
Bb7
dar - ling, and put all your dreams a -
1
Eb6
Ebdim
Edim
Bb7
way. Put your
2
Eb6
Ebdim
Fm7
Eb6/9
way.
8va
ppp
8va
Ped.

SAVED BY THE BELL

from the Television Series

Words and Music by
SCOTT GALE

D7
time. By the time I grab my books and give
F
myself a look, I'm at the corner just in time to see the
E
G
D/F♯
E
bus fly by. It's alright, 'cause I'm saved by the bell.
A
If the

D7
teach - er pops a test, I know I'm in a mess and my
Instrumental solo
fore I hes - i - tate, I'll ask her on a date, and we'll be
A
dog ate all my home - work last night. Rid - in'
go - in' out Sat - ur - day night. If she
D7
low in my chair, she won't know that I'm there. If I can
asks me to the dance, I won't stand a chance when she
F
E
hand it in to - mor - row, it 'll be al - right.
Solo ends
sees me out there mov - in' with my two left feet.

G
D/F♯
E
It's al - right, 'cause I'm saved by the bell.
A
To Coda
A7
D
A
Here comes that brown - eyed girl;
D
A
she looks so fine.

D
A
Ev - 'ry time I talk to her
F
E
G
D/F♯
E
I near - ly lose my mind.
It's al - right,
A
'cause I'm saved by the bell.
1
2
A7
D.S. al Coda
Be -

CODA
G
D/F#
E
It's al - right,
A
I said
G
D/F#
E
it's al - right,
A
yeah,
G
D/F#
E
it's al - right, 'cause I'm saved by the bell.

A
G
D/F#
E
It's al - right, 'cause I'm saved ___ by the...
it's al - right, 'cause I'm saved _ by the... it's al - right,
'cause I'm saved _ by the bell. ___

ROCKY & BULLWINKLE

from the Cartoon Television Series

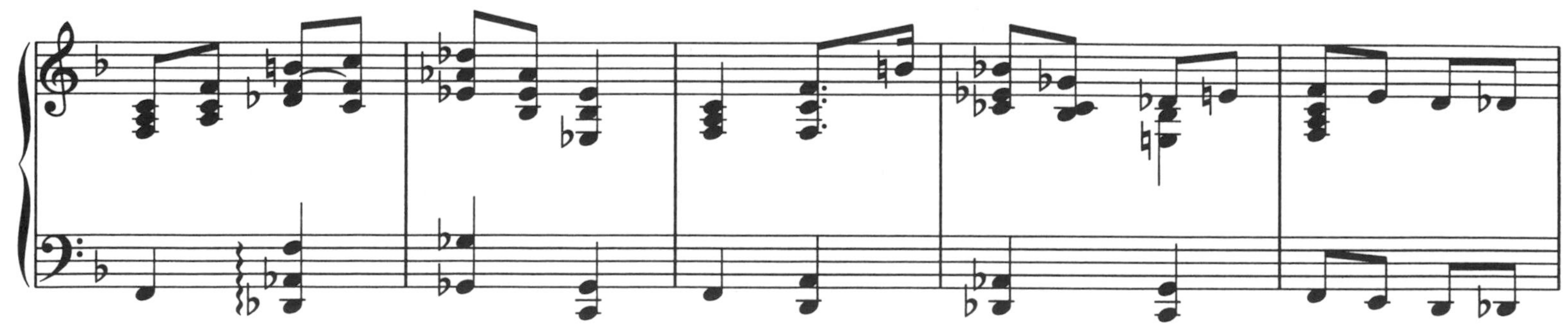

1
2

SEATTLE

from the Television Series HERE COME THE BRIDES

Words and Music by ERNIE SHELDON, JACK KELLER
and HUGO MONTENEGRO

Em D G D Em D Em D
hopes and full of fears, full of laugh - ter full of tears, full of dreams
G D C/E C D G D/F♯ Em7 C D
to last the years in Se - at - tle, in Se -
G D/F♯ To Coda G G Em
at - tle.
When it's time to leave your home and your
When you find your own true love you will
If you ev - er fall in love with a
C Am7 Am7/D D G Em
loved ones, it's the hard - est thing a girl boy can ev - er do.
know it, by his her smile, by the look in his her eye.
log - ger, there is some - thing you will have to un - der - stand.

F
D7
Am7/D
D
G
Em
And you pray that you will find some - one
Scent of pine trees in the air nev - er
For as much as he may care, you will
C
D7
C
D
C/E
D7/F♯
C/D
D
strong and good
warm and sweet
and kind,
but you're not sure what's wait - ing there for
knew a day so fair.
It makes you feel so good that you could
al - ways have to share,
his love with his green moun - tain
1,2
3
D.S. al Coda
G
G/D
G
G/D
you.
cry.
The blu - est sky
land.
The blu - est sky
CODA
G
D/F♯
Em7
G/D
G
C
G
In Se - at - tle,
in Se - at - tle.

SESAME STREET THEME

Words by BRUCE HART,
JON STONE and JOE RAPOSO
Music by JOE RAPOSO

B♭
F
C7
Dm7/C
C7
Dm7/C
how to get to Ses - a - me Street?
C
Dm7/C
C7
Dm7/C
A
It's a mag - ic car -
Bm7/A
E7/A
A
Bm7/A
E7
- pet ride.
Ev - 'ry door will o - pen wide to hap - py
A
E9/A
A
D9/A
D/A
A
peo - ple like you.
Hap - py peo - ple like...
What a beau - ti - ful

C F7 C
sun - ny day sweep - in' the clouds a -
F7 C F7 G7/D Dm7 G7/D
way. On my way to where the air is sweet.
G7 F9 G7/D B♭ F C Dm7/C
Can you tell me how to get, how to get to Ses - a - me Street?
C7 Dm7/C C Dm7/C C7 Dm7/C C7
How to get to Ses - a - me Street?

SEEMS LIKE OLD TIMES

from ARTHUR GODFREY AND HIS FRIENDS

Lyric and Music by JOHN JACOB LOEB
and CARMEN LOMBARDO

D7
G7
Gdim
G7
dawn, then dar - ling you were gone,
C7
Gm7
C7
Gm7
C7
Now it's al - most too good to be - lieve.
rall.
Moderately
(with feeling)
N.C.
D7+5
D7
D7+5
Seems like old times, hav - ing you to
G9
G7
walk with, seems like old times, hav - ing you to

Gm7
C7-9
talk with. And it's still a thrill just to
F6
D7+5
G9
G7
have my arms a - round you, Still the
C7
N.C.
thrill that it was the day I found you, Seems like
D7+5
D7
D7+5
old times, din - ner dates and

G9 G7

flow - ers, Just like old times, stay - ing up for

Gm7 C7-9

ho - urs, Mak - ing dreams come true, do - ing

F6 D7+5 D7 G9 Gm7 C9 C7-9

things we used to do, Seems like old times, ___ be - ing here with

1 F Fdim B♭dim F N.C. 2 F B♭ F

you. Seems like you. ___

mf *rall.* ***p***

SOLID GOLD

Theme from the Television Series SOLID GOLD

Words by DEAN PITCHFORD
Music by MICHAEL K. MILLER

G♭/B♭
6 fr
A♭/B♭
B♭no3rd
you let the songs take con - trol.
heat keeps me warm when I'm cold.
B♭m
F/B♭
The sound starts to glis - sten, the
The beat starts to bend me, the
D♭/B♭
7 fr
E♭/B♭
6 fr
more that you lis - ten, and
mel - o - dies send me, and
G♭/B♭
6 fr
A♭/B♭
B♭sus
slow - ly it turns in - to gold.
ev - 'ry - thing melts in - to gold.

B♭
B♭/A♭
G♭maj7
Sol - id gold,
fill - ing up
F7♯5
F7
B♭m
B♭m/A♭
G♭maj7
my life with mu - sic.
Sol - id gold,
put - ting
rhy - thm in my soul.
B♭m
B♭sus
B♭
E♭m
There's a song that's un -

Fm7
Db/F
Gb
reel - ing to fit the way that I'm feel -
Fm7
Db/F
Ebm7
Fm7
Gb
- ing; my head keeps spin - ning to mu -
Ab
4 fr
Bbsus
1
- sic spin - ning to gold. I've
2
Fm
Ab
4 fr
Bbm
So - lid gold!

THEME FROM "STAR TREK®"

from the Paramount Television Series STAR TREK

Words by GENE RODDENBERRY
Music by ALEXANDER COURAGE

Bright Galactic Beguine

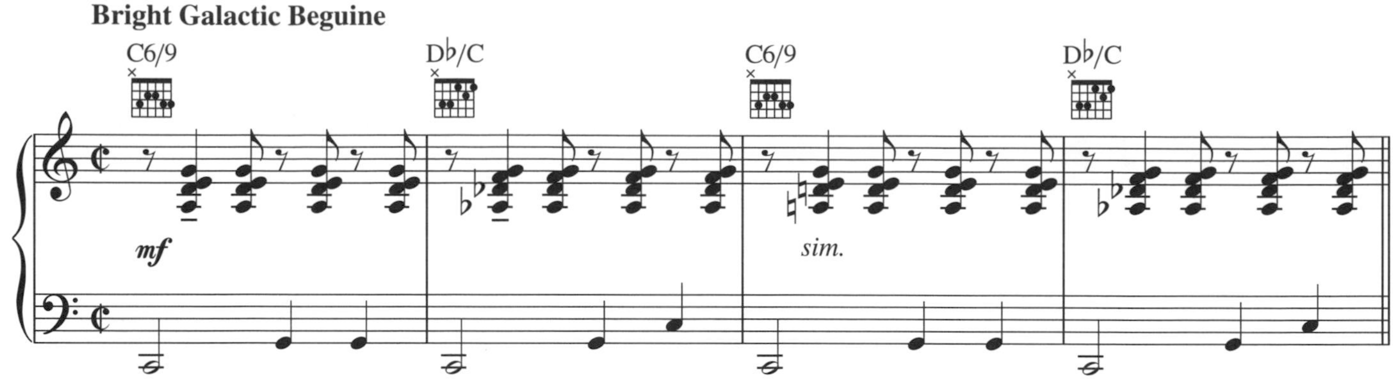

E♭
3fr
D6
3
I know he'll find, in star - clus - tered
D♭9
D♭13♯11
4fr
E♭6
3
reach - es, love, strange love a star - wom - an
G7♯5(♯9)
3fr
G7♯5
C(add2)
3
teach - es. I know his jour - ney ends
A♭13
3fr
C6/9
nev - er; His star trek

F9♯11
E9
E9♭5
6fr
will go on for - ev - er.
But
F6
B♭9♯11
C6/9
tell him while he wan - ders his star - ry
A7♯5(♭9)
Dm7
Dm7/G
sea, Re - mem - ber, re - mem - ber
C6/9
D♭/C
C6/9
me.

STAR TREK - DEEP SPACE NINE®

Theme from the Paramount Television Series STAR TREK: DEEP SPACE NINE

By DENNIS McCARTHY

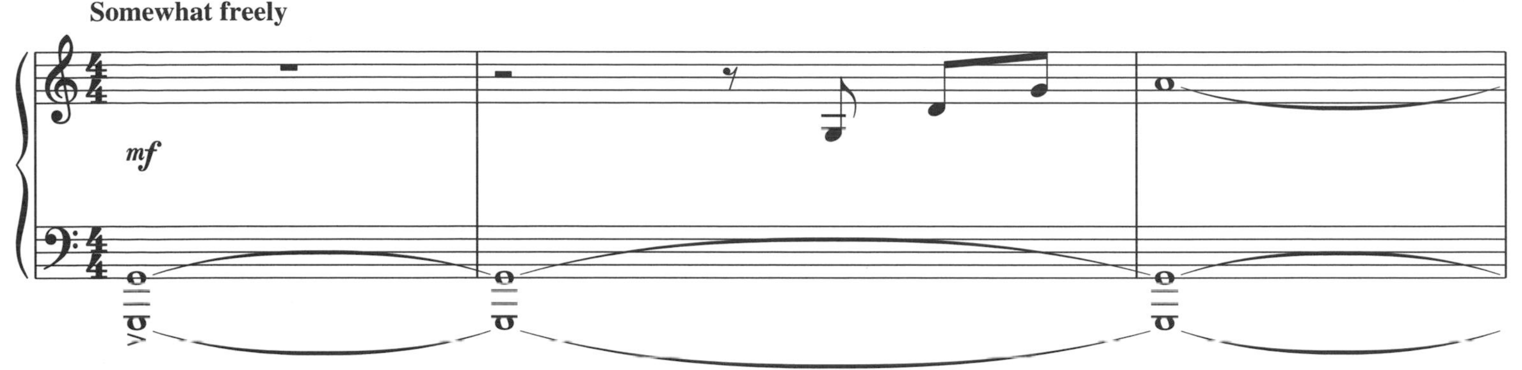

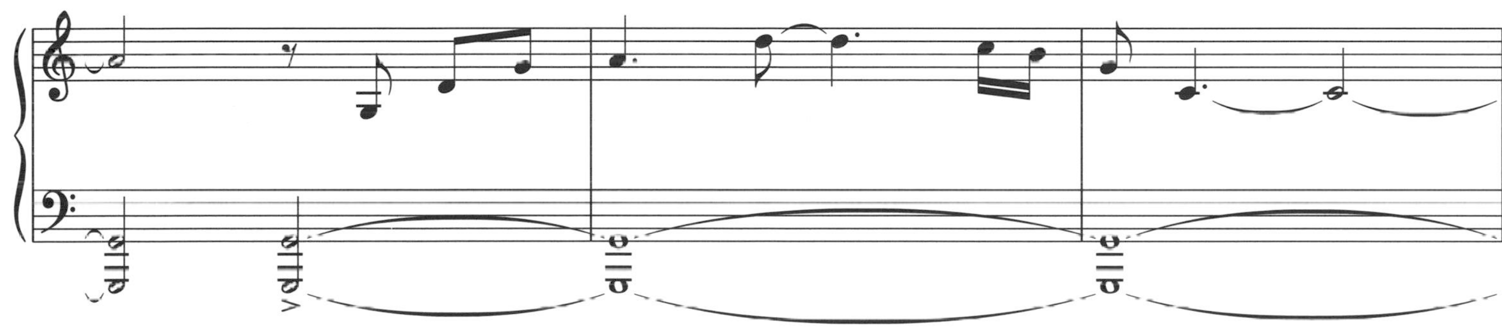

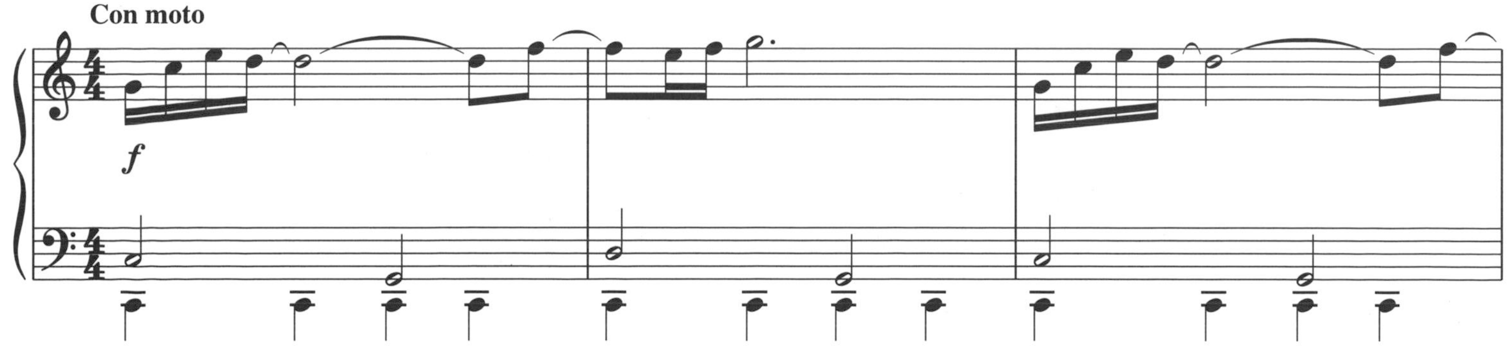

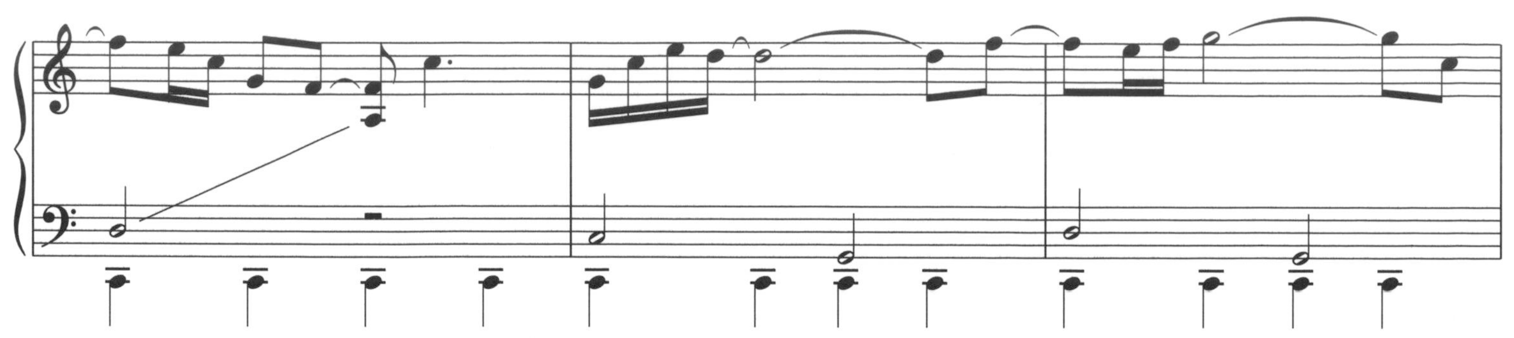

mf

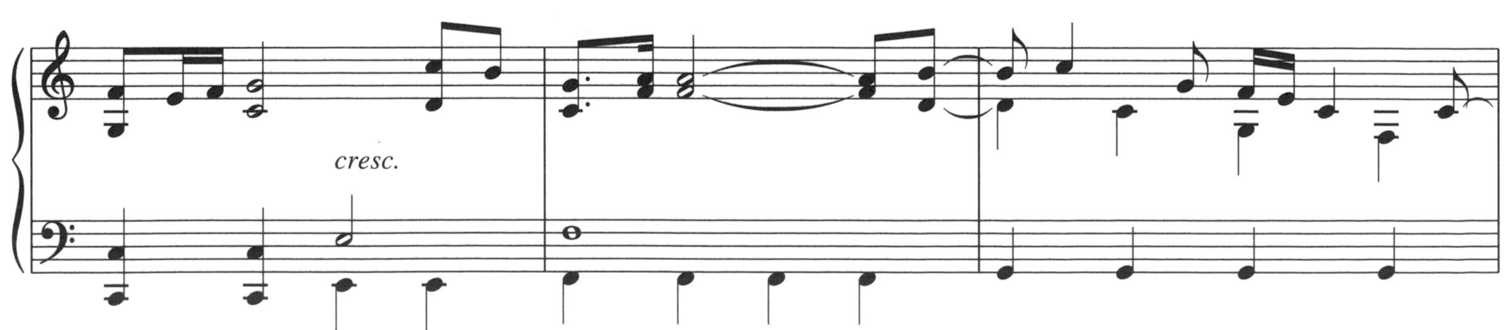
cresc.

f

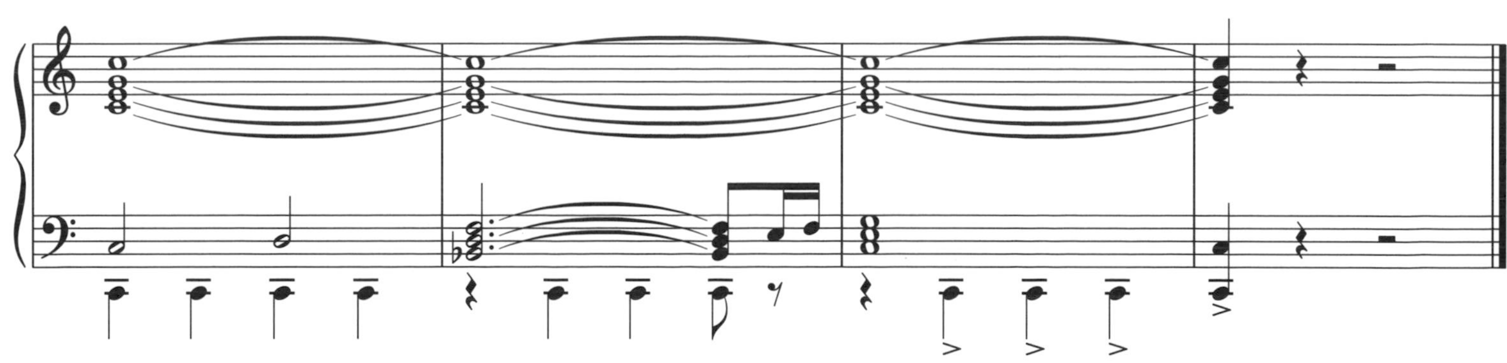

STAR TREK-THE NEXT GENERATION®

Theme from the Paramount Television Series STAR TREK: THE NEXT GENERATION

By ALEXANDER COURAGE,
GENE RODDENBERRY and JERRY GOLDSMITH

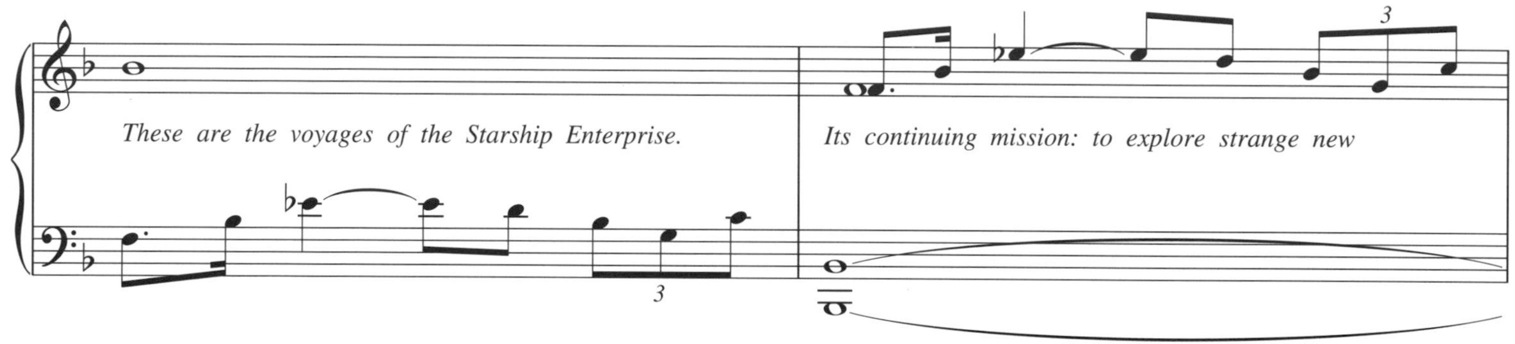

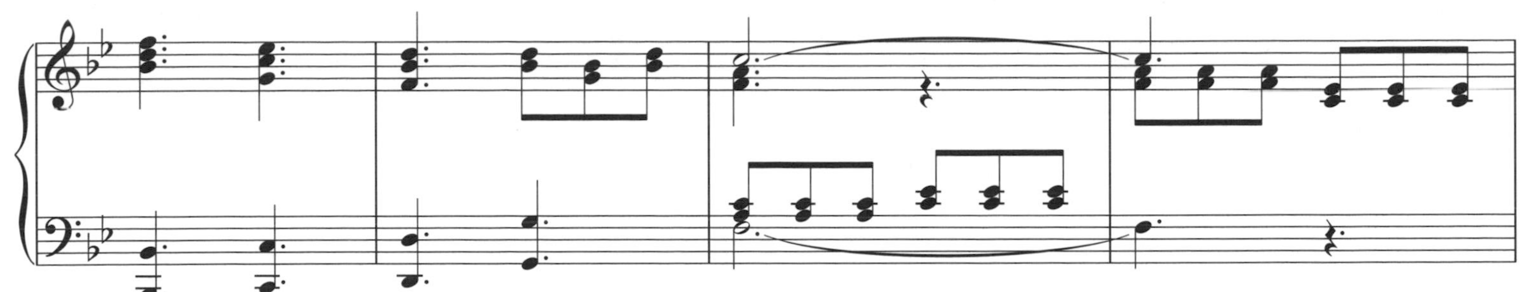

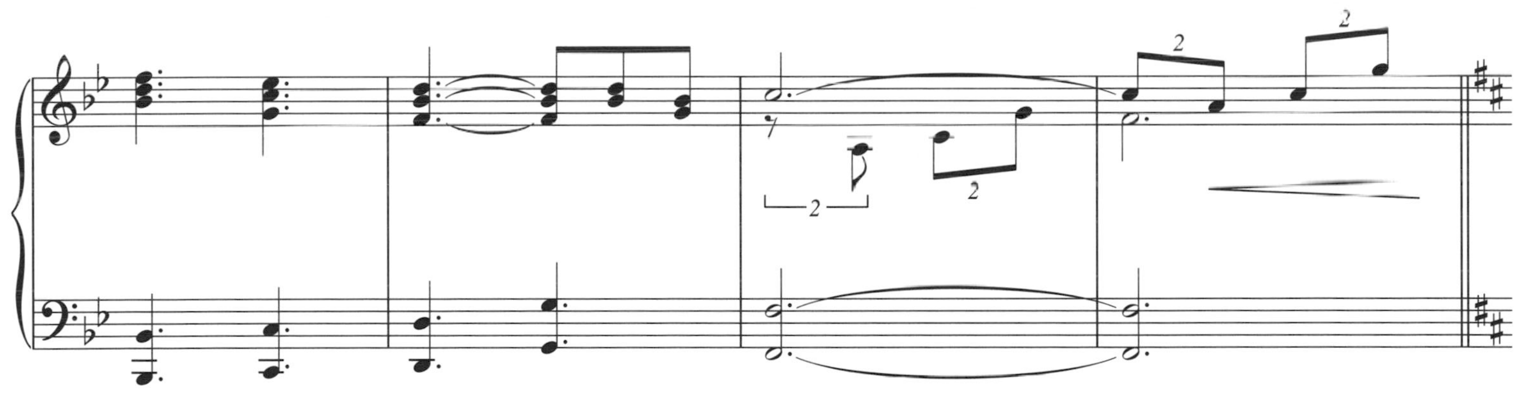

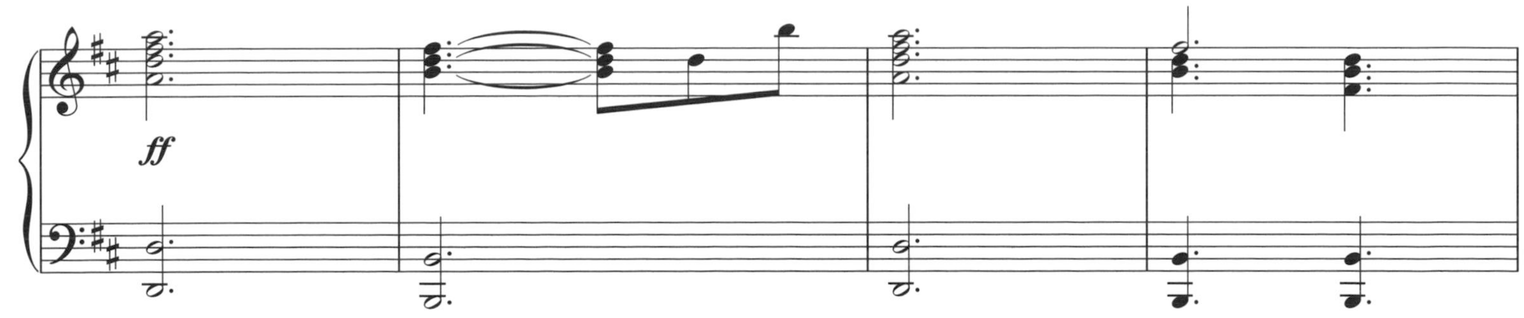
ff

2
2

f

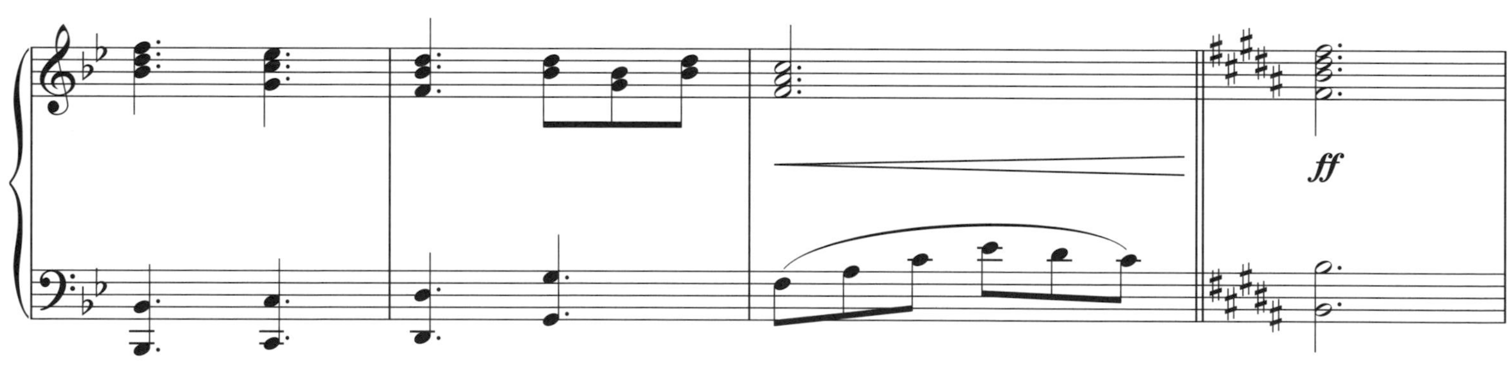
ff

f
ff

STAR TREK - VOYAGER®

Theme from the Paramount Television Series STAR TREK: VOYAGER

Music by JERRY GOLDSMITH

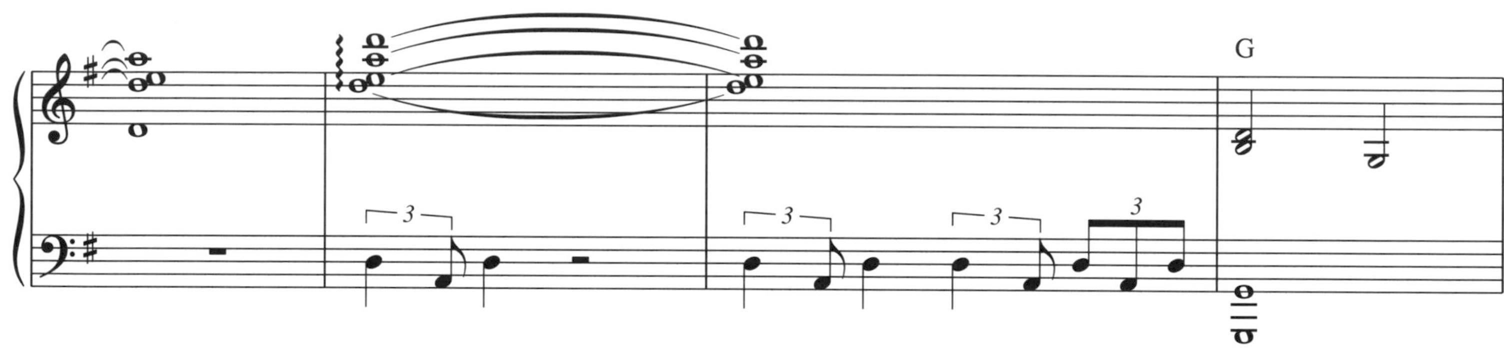

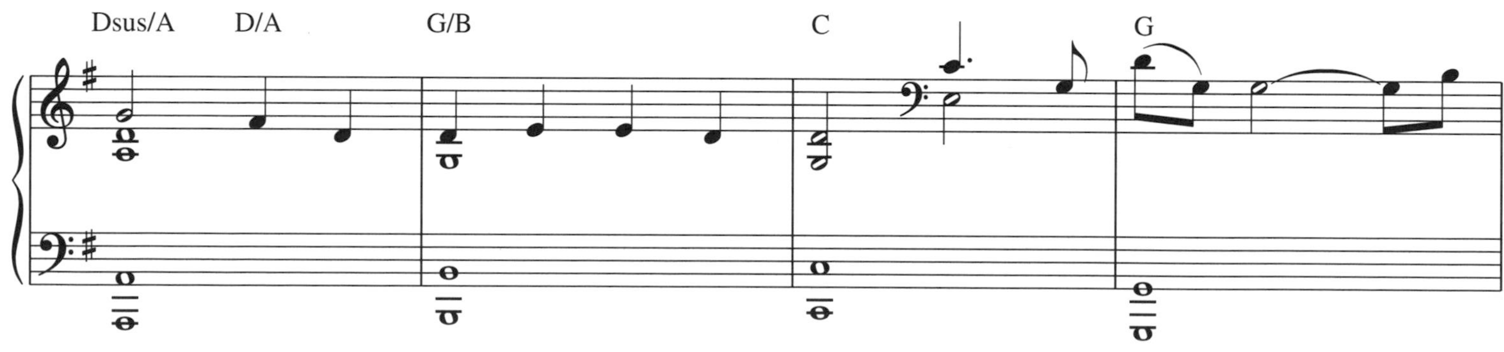

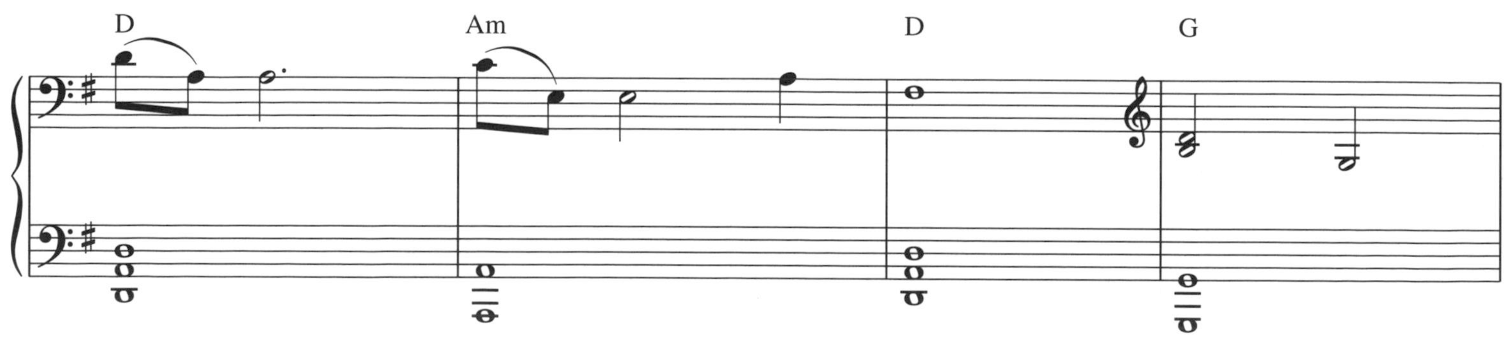

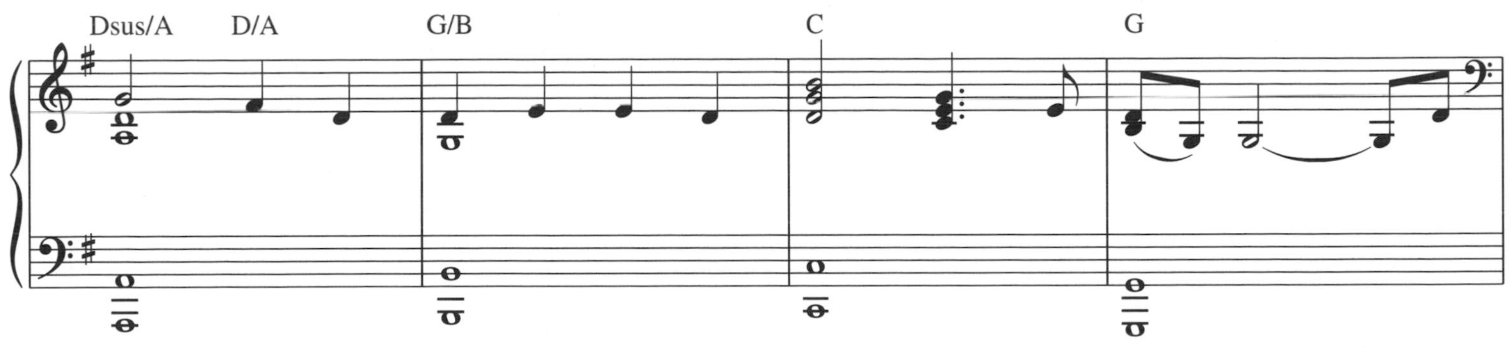
Dsus/A
D/A
G/B
C
G

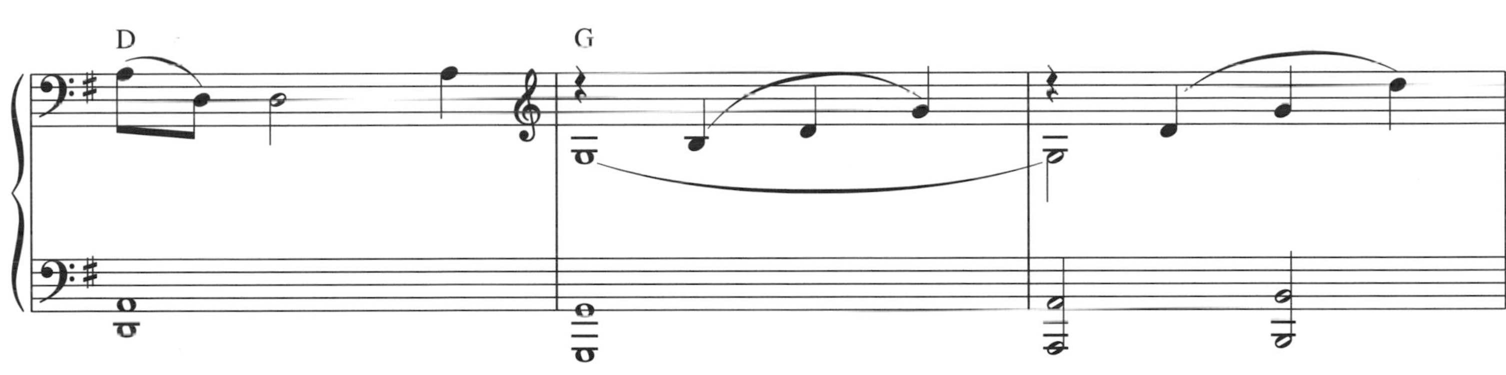
D
G

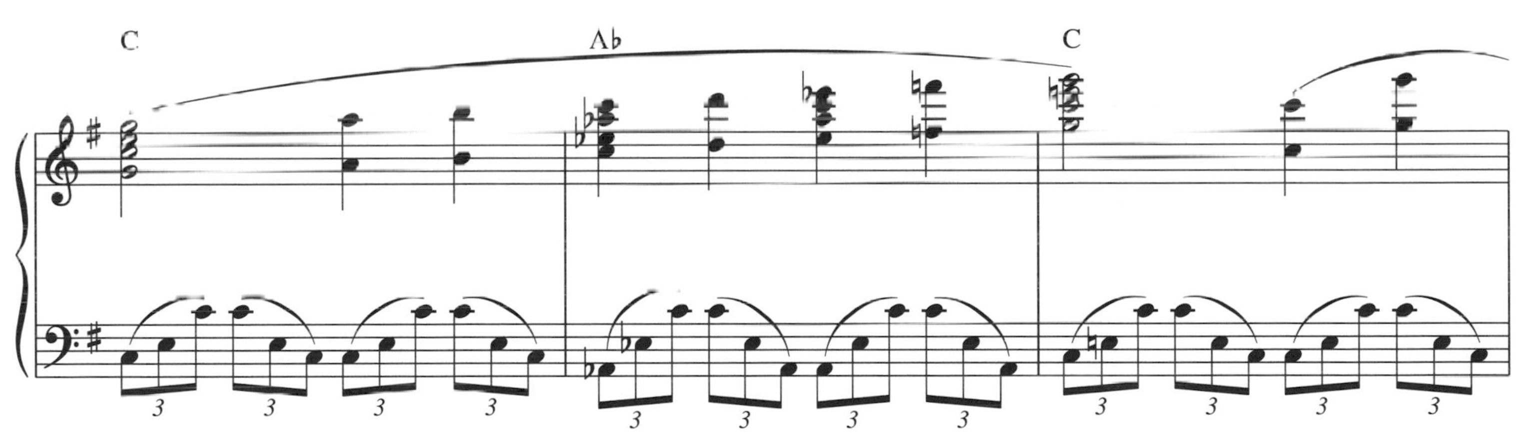
C
A♭
C

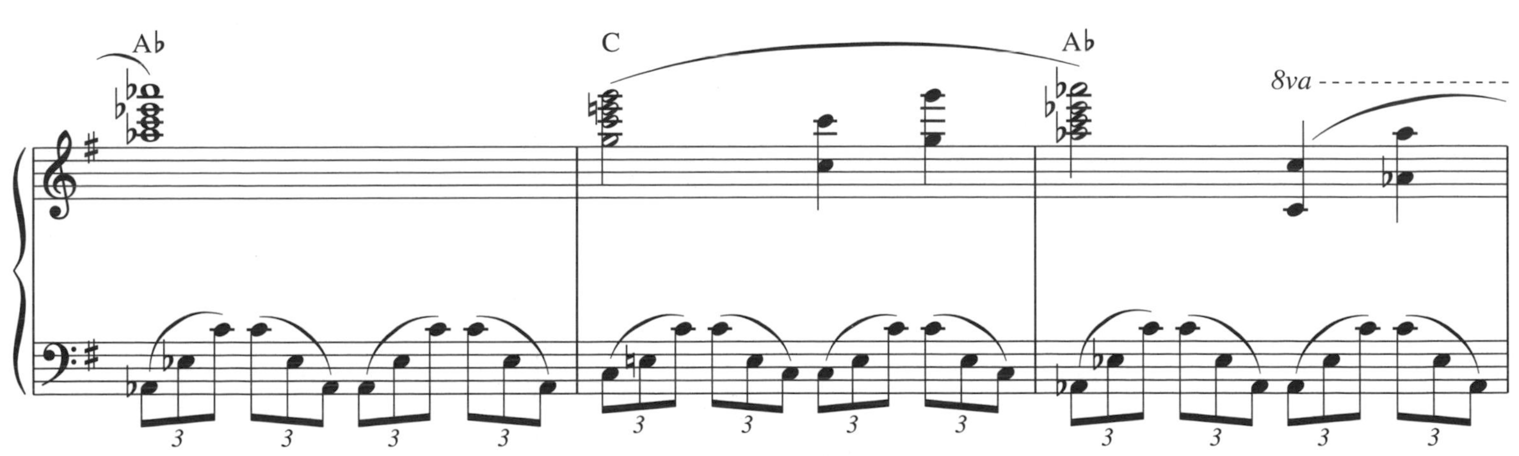
A♭
C
A♭
8va

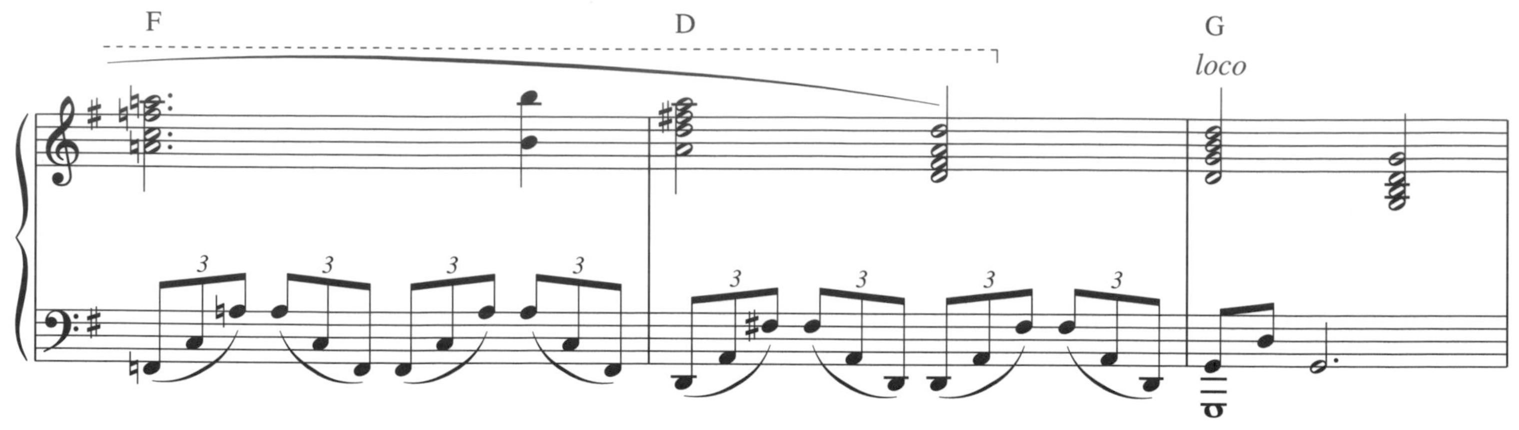
F
D
G
loco
3

Dsus/A
D/A
G/B
C

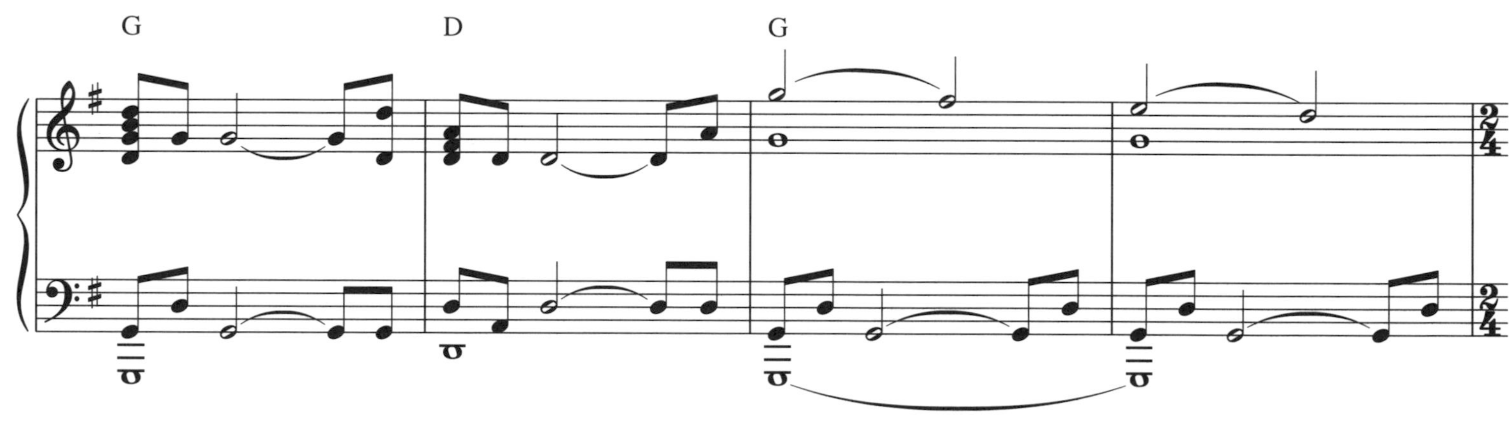
G
D
G

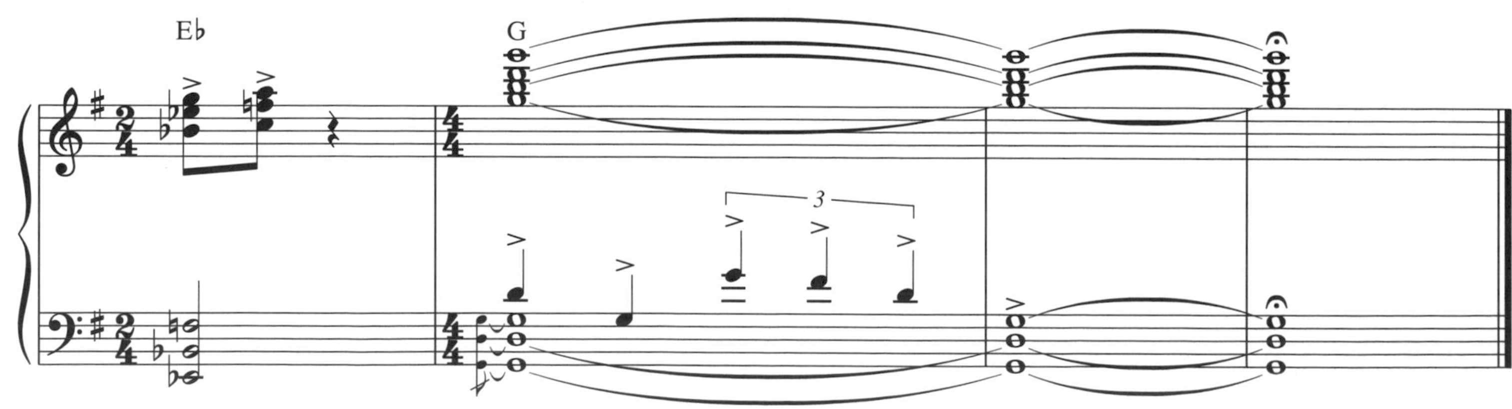
E♭
G
3

THEN CAME YOU

from the Paramount TV Series WEBSTER

Words by MADELINE SUNSHINE
Music by STEVEN D. NELSON

G
Dm7
F
C
Set in my ways, losing track of the days; never getting caught up.
Eb6
G/D
Dsus
D
3
Love was never brought up; it's not the thing to do. Ooh,
cresc.
Fmaj9/G
C/E
D
G/D
it was you; then came you. You made me leap without
f
Am/D
G/D
D
Fmaj9/G
C/E
takin' a look. Ooh, it was you; then came you. You

D
G/D
Am/D
G/D
D
Am7
reeled me right in, line, sink - er and hook. I nev - er thought for - ev - er was the
Dsus
D
Fmaj9/G
best I could do; then came you. It was you
C/G
F/G
C/G
G
and me and you. It was you and me and
Csus/G
C/G
F/G
C/G
G
you. It was you and me and then came you.

THIRTYSOMETHING
(Main Title Theme)
from the Television Series

By W.G. SNUFFY WALDEN
and STEWART LEVIN

E♭/G
A♭
B♭
B♭sus
B♭
E♭
3
B♭
B♭7/D
E♭sus
E♭
B♭
B♭7/D
E♭sus
E♭
B♭/D
Cm7
F7

To Coda
Bb7
Bb
Eb
Cm7
Db(add9)
Bbsus
Bb/D
Eb
Cm7
Db(add9)
Eb/G
Ab

E♭/G
A♭
E♭
A♭/C
B♭/D
E♭
A♭/C
B♭/D
E♭
E♭/G
A♭
R.H.
B♭
B♭/D
E♭
Fm7

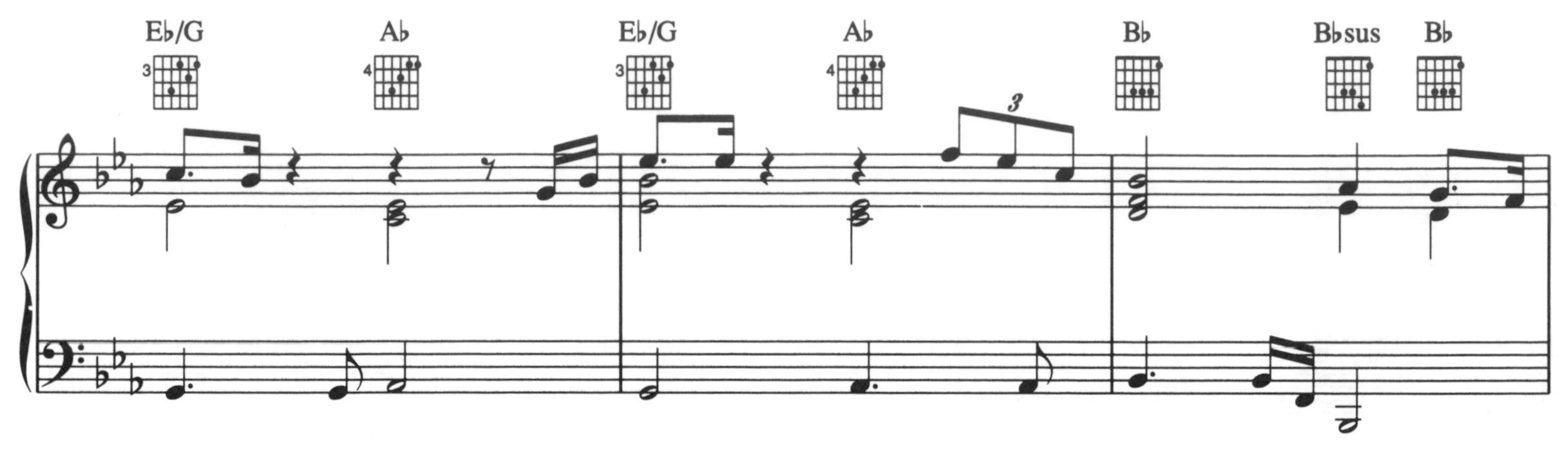
Eb/G
Ab
Eb/G
Ab
Bb
Bbsus
Bb

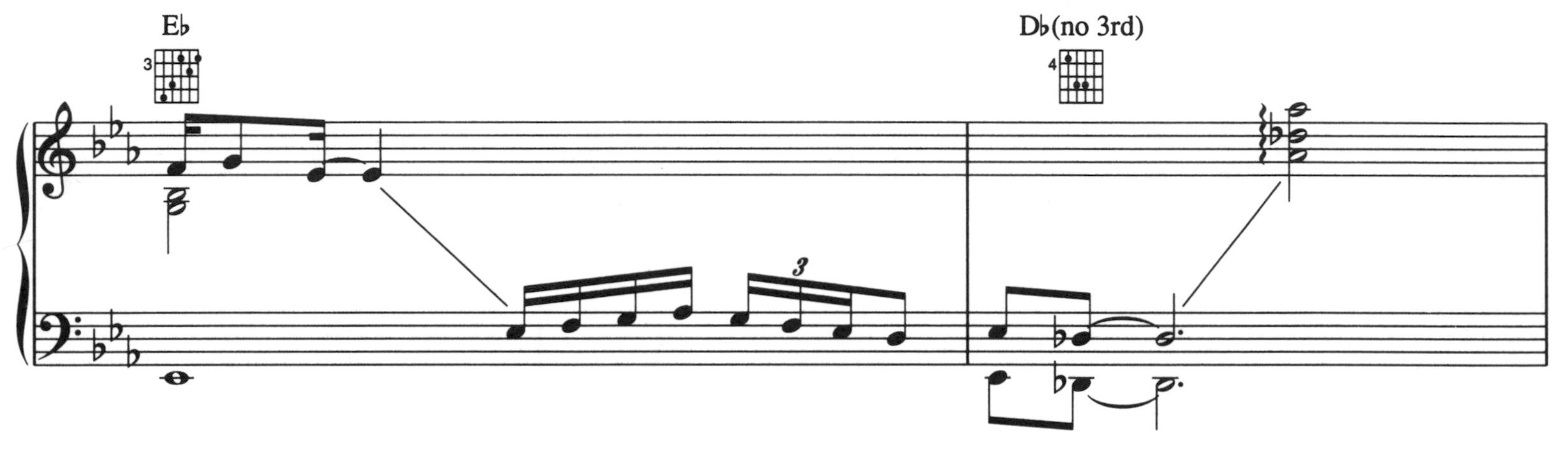
Eb
Db(no 3rd)

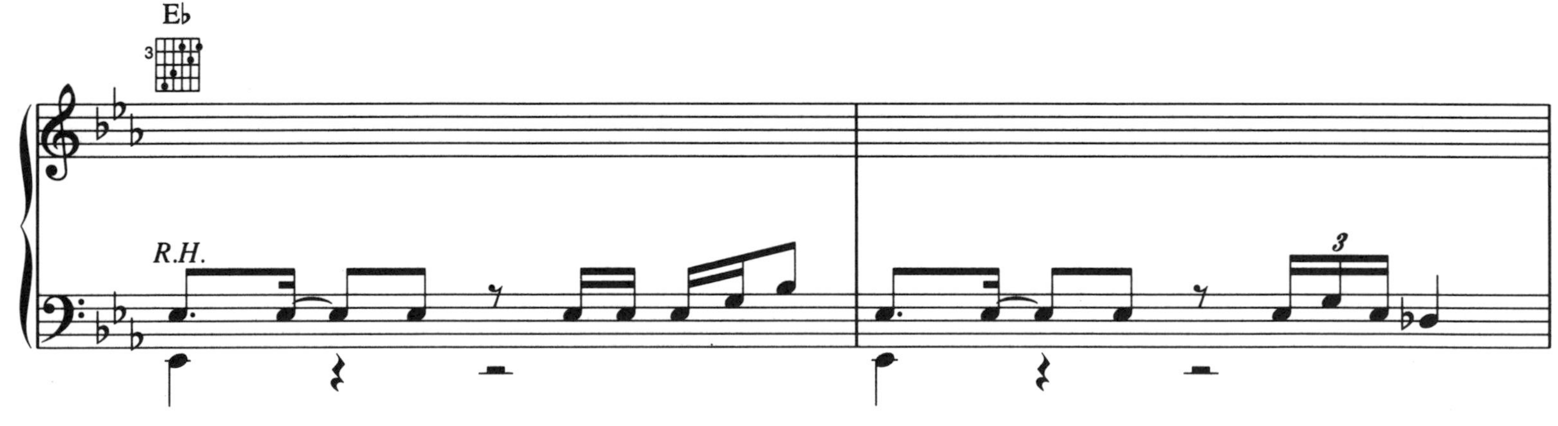
Eb
R.H.

Eb/G
Ab
Bbsus
Ab
Bbm
Ab/C
8va
Bb
Cm7
Bb/D
Db
Eb/G
Ab
Eb/G
Ab

B♭sus
D.S. al Coda
CODA
E♭/G
A♭
B♭
B♭/D
E♭
Fm7
E♭/G
A♭
E♭/G
A♭
B♭
B♭7sus
B♭
E♭

THREE'S COMPANY THEME

from the Television Series

Words by JOE RAPOSO and DON NICHOLL
Music by JOE RAPOSO

D9 5 fr.
G7
G♯dim
Gm7
Gm7/C
) We've a lov-a-ble space that needs your face, Three's com - pan-y, too.
F
N.C.
F
Come and knock on our door, (Come and knock on our door,
Am7 5 fr.
D9 5 fr.
) We've been wait-ing for you, (We've been wait-ing for you,) Where the kiss-es are hers
G7
G♯dim
Gm7
Gm7/C
F
E♭maj7 3 fr.
C9
and hers are his, Three's com - pan-y, too.

F
Bm7
7fr.
E7 -9 +5
8fr.
Am7
5fr.
D7 -9 +5
6fr.
You'll see that life is a ball__ a-gain, laugh-ter is call - in' for
Gm11
N.C.
Bbmaj7/C
5fr.
you.
Down at our ren-dez-vous__
(Down at our ren - dez - vous__
C11
1.
F
) Three is com - pan - y, too.
N.C.
2.
F
Ebmaj7
3 fr.
C9
F
Come and dance on our floor,

THE TOY PARADE

Theme from LEAVE IT TO BEAVER

By D. KAHN,
M. LENARD and M. GREENE

Gm
C
F
Gm
ging - ham cat in a sol - dier's hat is wav - ing a chi - nese
C
F
Gm
C
fan, a plas - tic clown in a wed - ding gown is
F
C7
F
F#7
B7♭5
B♭7
A7
danc - ing with Rag - ge - dy Ann. Fee fie
Dm
fid - dle dee dee they're cross - ing the liv - ing room floor,

G7
C7
fee fie fid - dle dee dee they're up to the din - ing room
F
Gm
C
door. They call a halt for a choc - 'late malt or
F
Gm
Gm7
C9
F
cook - ies and lem - on - ade, then off they go with a
Gm
C
F
C7
A♭6
G7
G♭maj7
F
ho ho ho right back to their toy pa - rade.

THEME FROM "THE UNTOUCHABLES"

from THE UNTOUCHABLES

By NELSON RIDDLE

With strong, steady movement

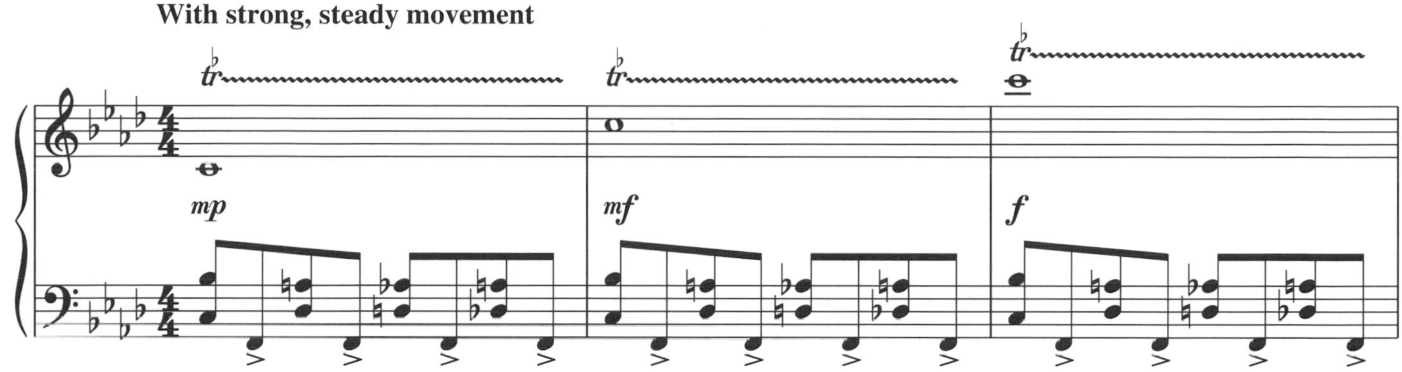

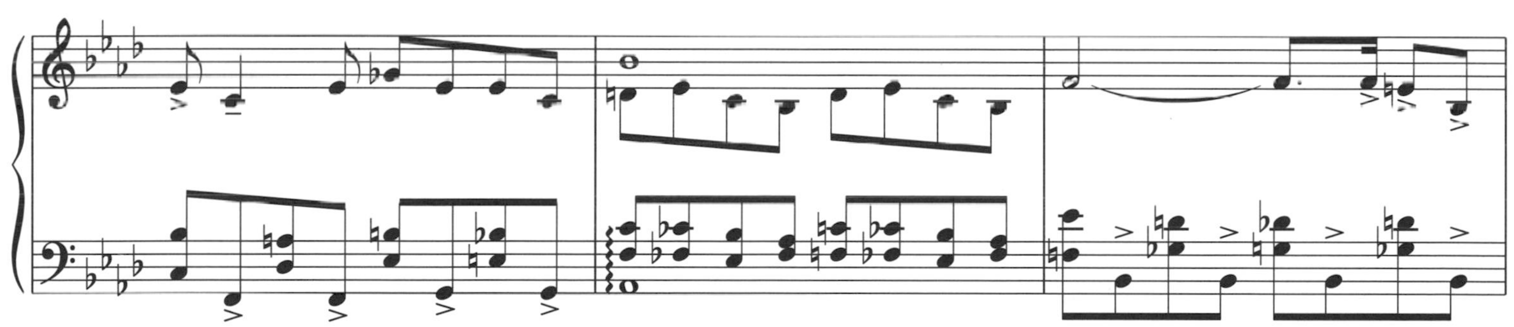

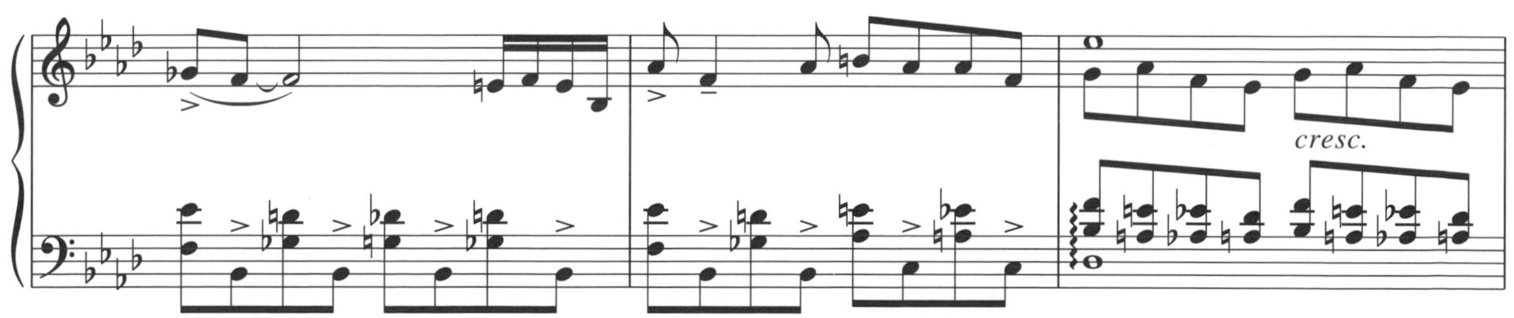

f

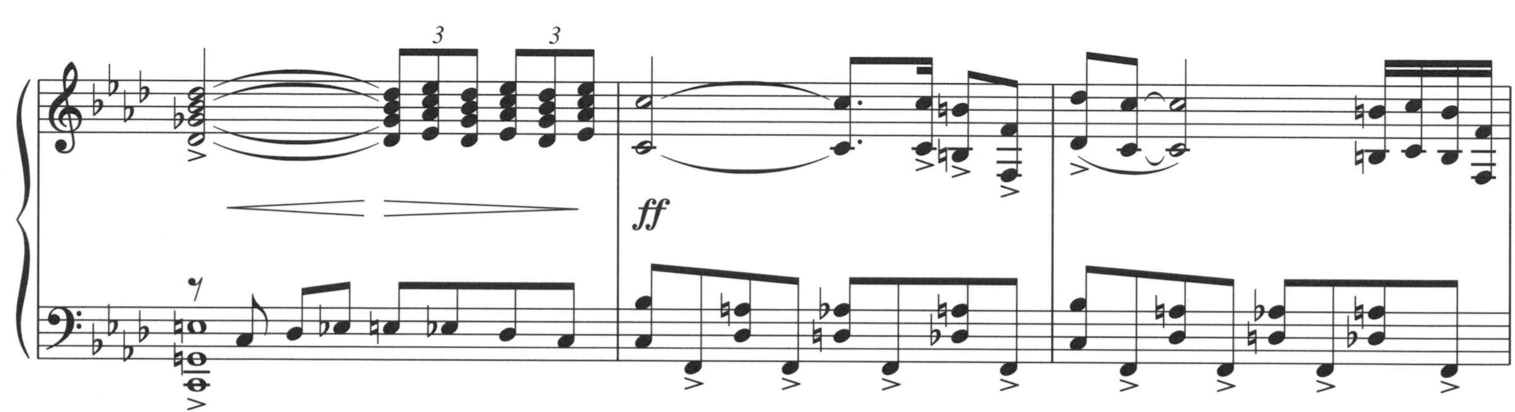
3
3
ff

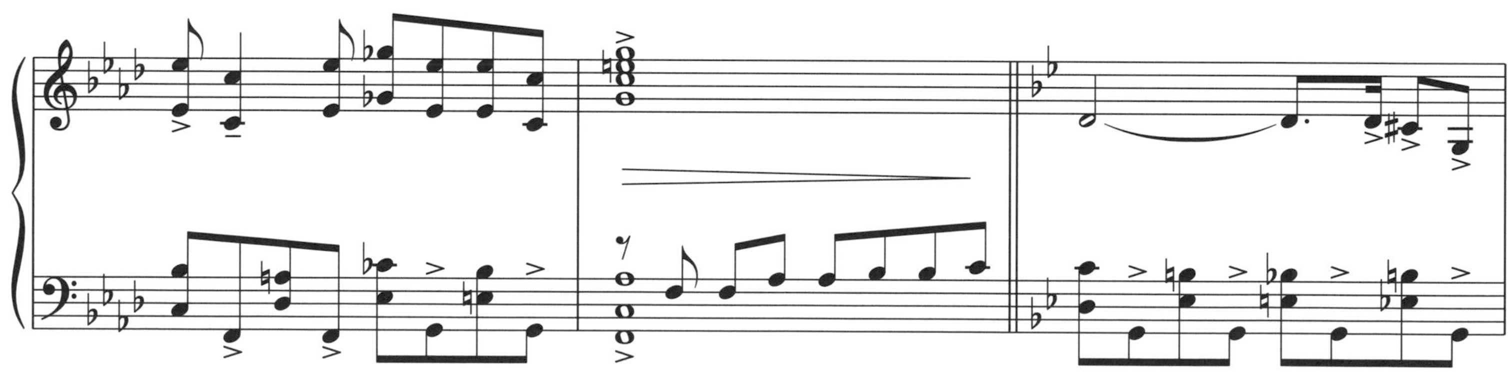

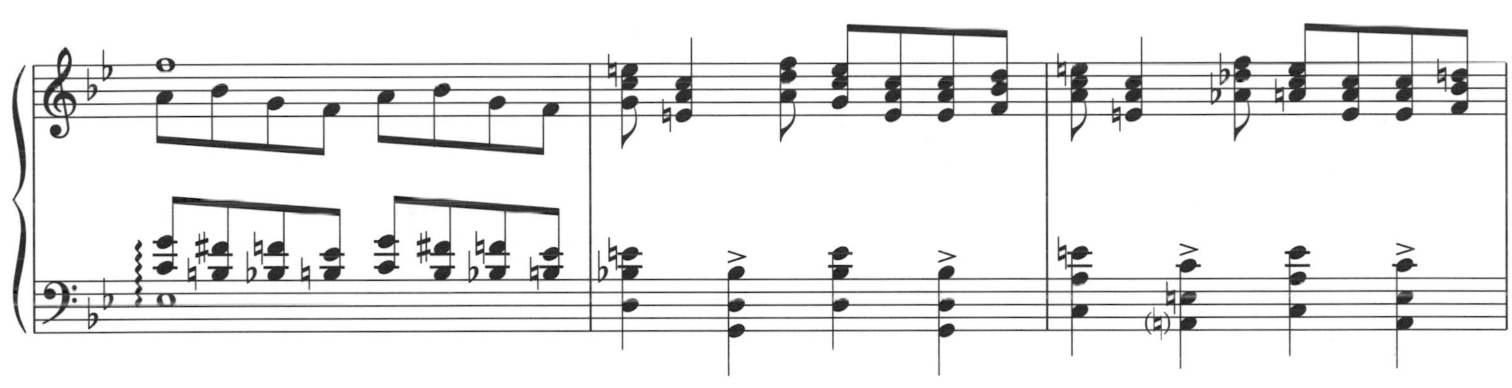

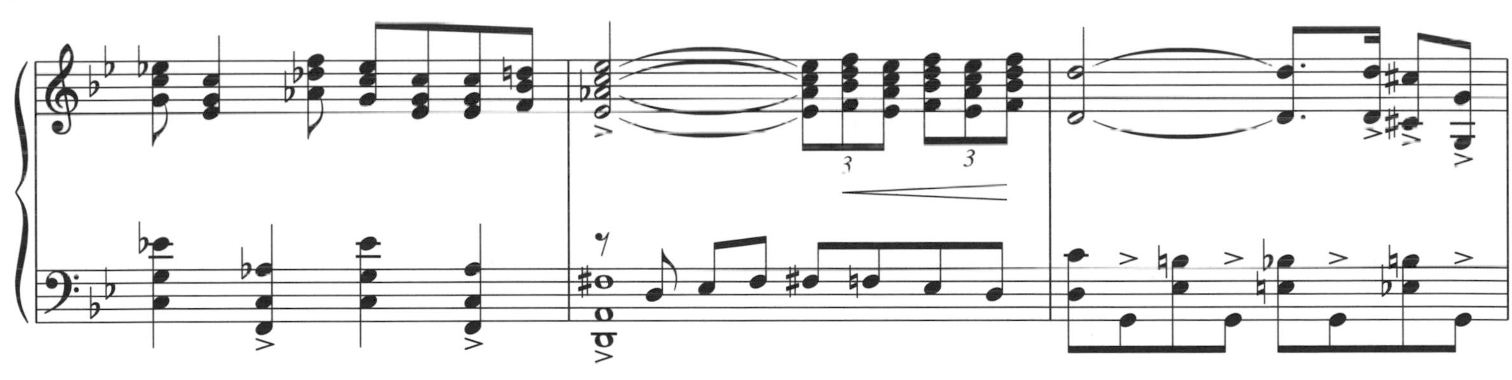

molto rit.

WHERE EVERYBODY KNOWS YOUR NAME

Theme from the Paramount Television Series CHEERS

Words and Music by GARY PORTNOY
and JUDY HART ANGELO

Eb/F
Bb
Ab
4fr
Some-times you wan-na go where ev-'ry-bod-y knows your
f
Eb
3fr
F
Gm7
F/A
name,
and they're al ways glad you came.
Dm
You wan-na be where you can see our
troub-les are all the same.
You wan-na be where ev-'ry-bod-y knows

Bb
F/Bb
Dm
Eb
3fr
your name.
You wan-na go _ where peo - ple know
Dm
Eb
3fr
Dm
Eb
3fr
F
peo-ple are all the same. ___
You wan-na go ___ where ev-'ry-bod-y knows
dim.
1
Bb
F/Bb
Bb
F/Bb
your name.
2
Bb
F/Bb
Bb
F/Bb
Bb
your name.
rit.

YOU LOOK AT ME

Theme from the Paramount TV Series JOANIE LOVES CHACHI

Words by PAMELA PHILLIPS OLAND and JIM DUNNE
Music by JIM DUNNE

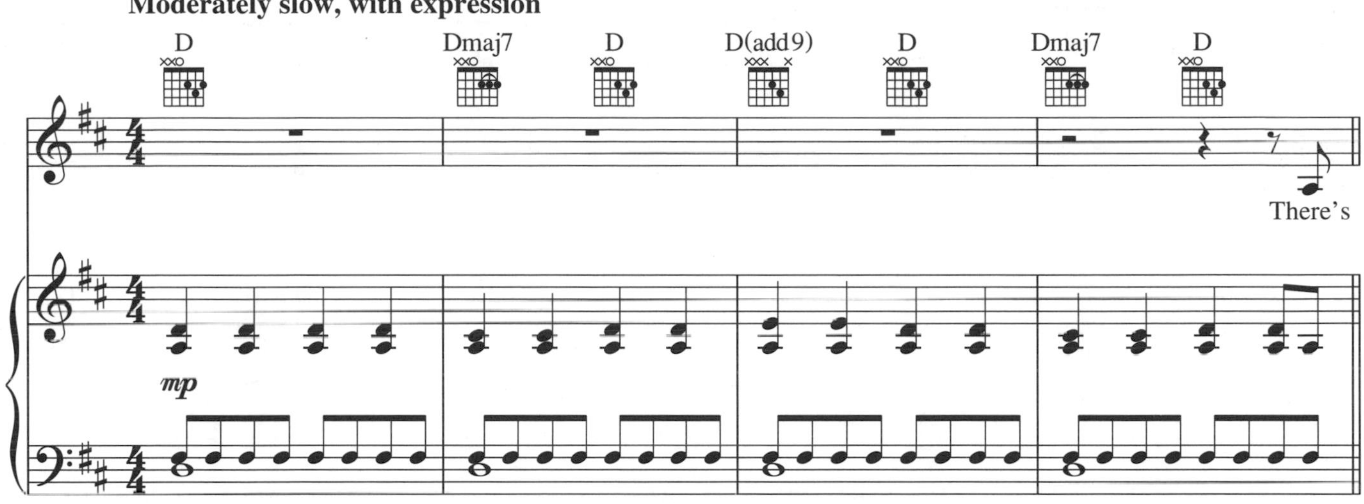

Em7/A
A7
Em7/A
A7
D
don't know what's come o - ver me. You've got me hyp - no - tized, when you look at me.
Dmaj7
D
D(add9)
D
Dmaj7
D
This feel - ing's not like an - y - thing I've known be - fore. You're
G
B♭6
D/A
all I dreamed that love would be, and so much more. I can't be - lieve it's true: you
G♯m7♭5
Gmaj7/A
A7
Em7/A
A7
feel the way I do, when you look at me. You
cresc.

D(add9)
D
Bm7
Bm(maj7)
Bm
Em7
Em7/D
look at me, soft as an - y touch could be, and sud - den - ly, there's
mf
Em7/A
A7
Em7/A
A7
D
mag - ic, when you look at me. I feel like I'm in
Bm7
Bm(maj7)
Bm
G
G/F#
Em7
Em7/A
heav - en, ev - 'ry mo - ment when you look at me. You
D
Bm7
Bm(maj7)
Bm
Em7
look at me.

Em7/A A7 Em7/A A7 D Bm7 Bm(maj7) Bm
G Em7 Em7/A D
You look at — me, soft —
cresc.
f
Bm7 Bm(maj7) Bm G
— as an - y touch — could be and sud - den - ly, — there's
Em7/A A7 Em7/A A7 D B♭
mag - ic, when you look at — me, and I can see

D
A/C♯
Bm
E7
G
love in your eyes.
You look at me, and
Gm7
D
A/C♯
Bm
Bm7
Bm7/E
E7
N.C.
mag - i - c'lly, I'm cap - tured in your eyes.
You
rit.
mp
D
Bm7
Em
Em7/A
A7
D
look at me, you look at me; there's mag - ic in your eyes.
a tempo
rit.

WILLIAM TELL OVERTURE

featured in the TV Series THE LONE RANGER

By G. ROSSINI

Bb7
Eb
3 fr
Eb+
Ab
4 fr
Eb
3 fr
Bb7
Eb
3 fr
Fm/Ab
F/A
Bb
Bb7
Eb
3 fr
Eb+
Ab
4 fr
Eb
3 fr
N.C.
Bb7
Eb
3 fr

WINGS

Theme from the Paramount Television Series WINGS

"Sonata In A" by FRANZ SCHUBERT
as Adapted and Arranged by ANTONY COOKE

mf
dim. poco a poco
mp
mf
poco rall.

WITH A LITTLE HELP FROM MY FRIENDS

featured in THE WONDER YEARS

Words and Music by JOHN LENNON
and PAUL McCARTNEY

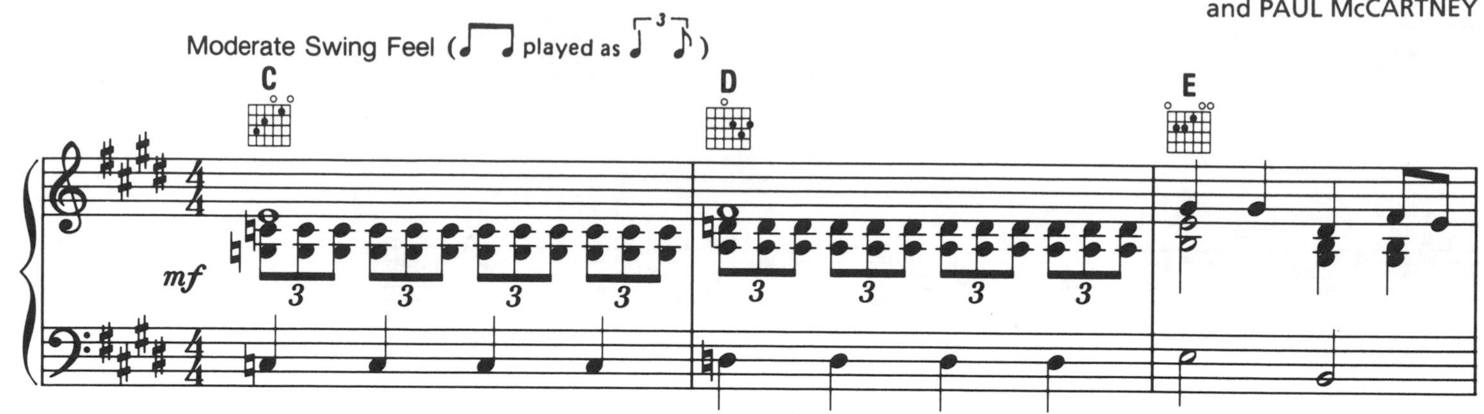

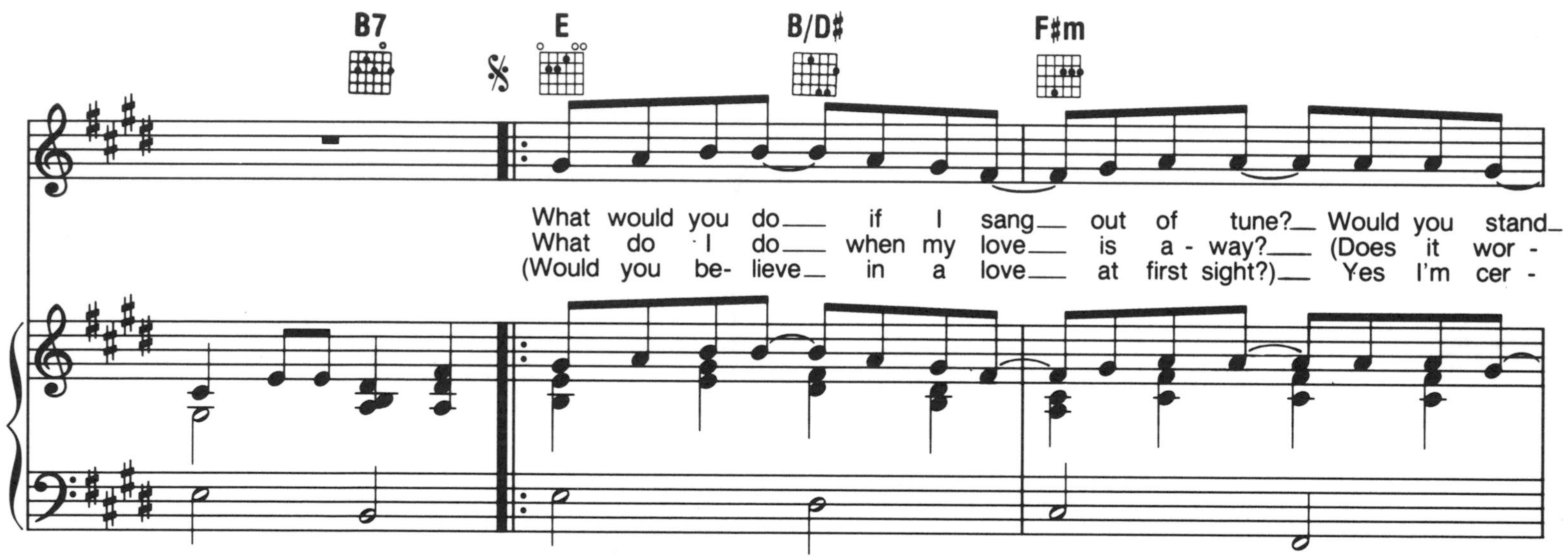

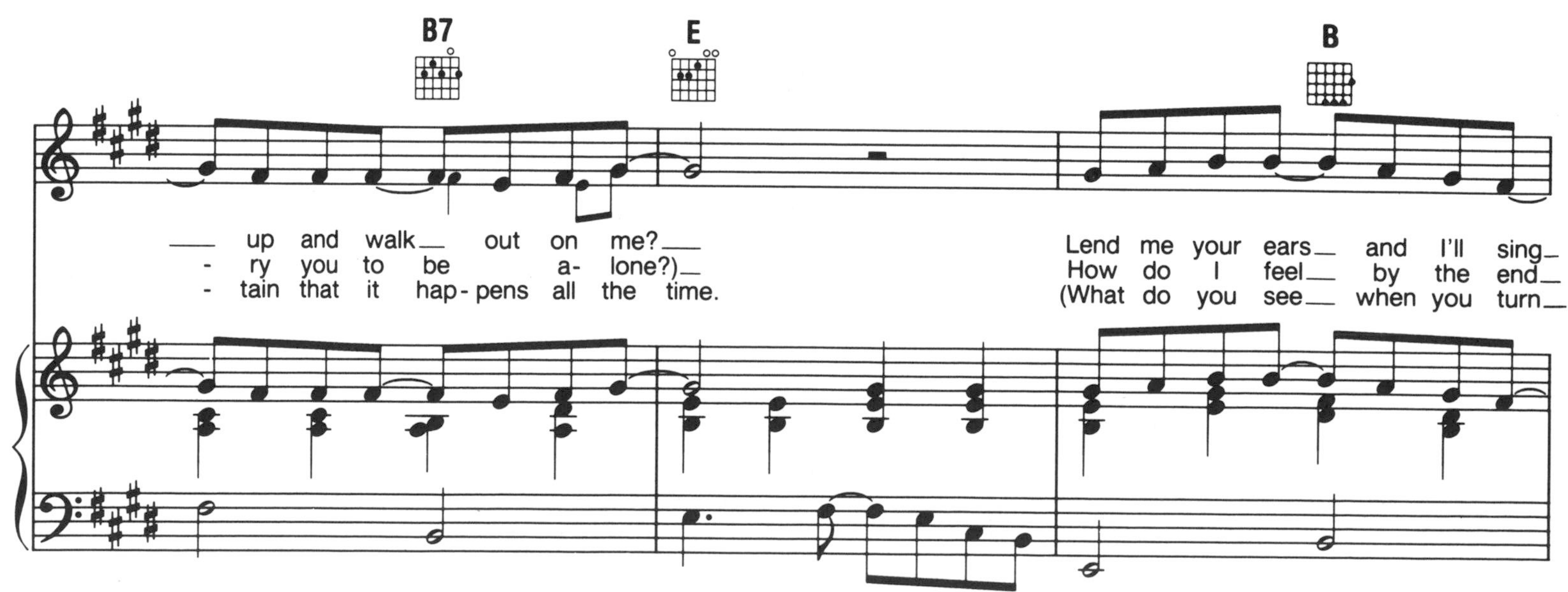

F♯m
B7
you a song and I'll try not to sing out of key.
of the day? (Are you sad be - cause you're on your own?)
out the light?) I can't tell you, but I know it's mine.

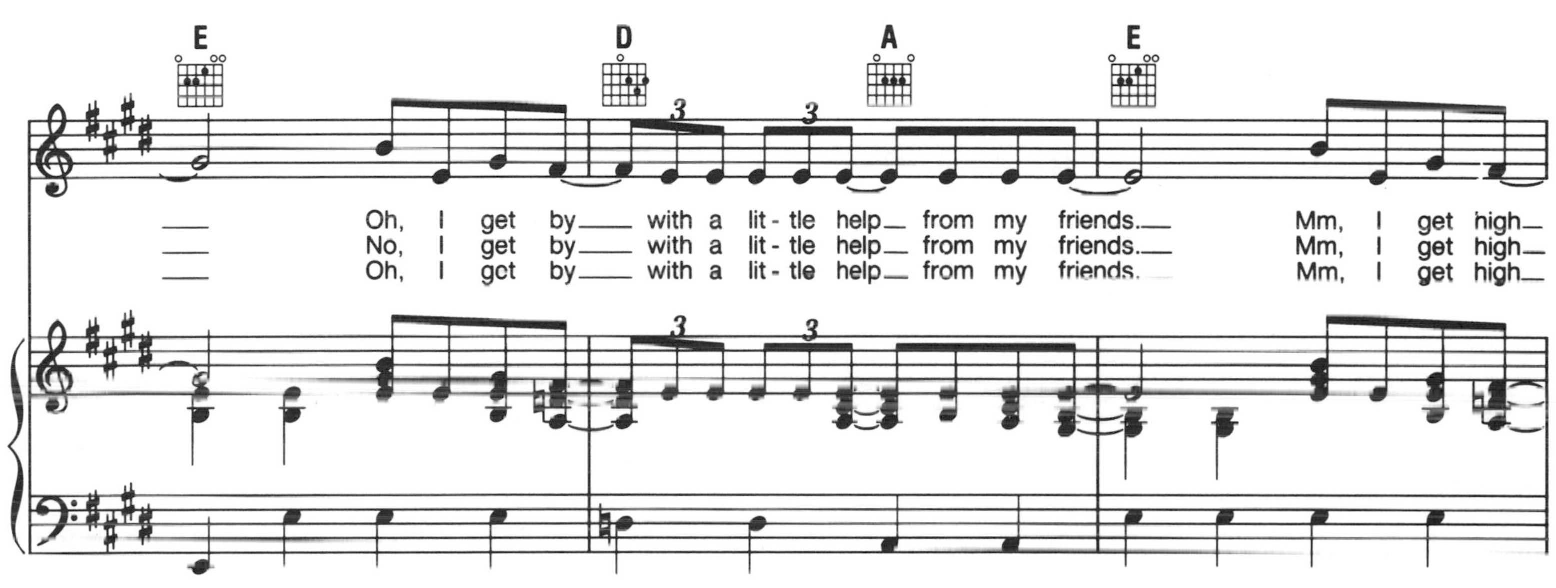
E
D
A
E
Oh, I get by with a lit - tle help from my friends. Mm, I get high
No, I get by with a lit - tle help from my friends. Mm, I get high
Oh, I get by with a lit - tle help from my friends. Mm, I get high
3
3

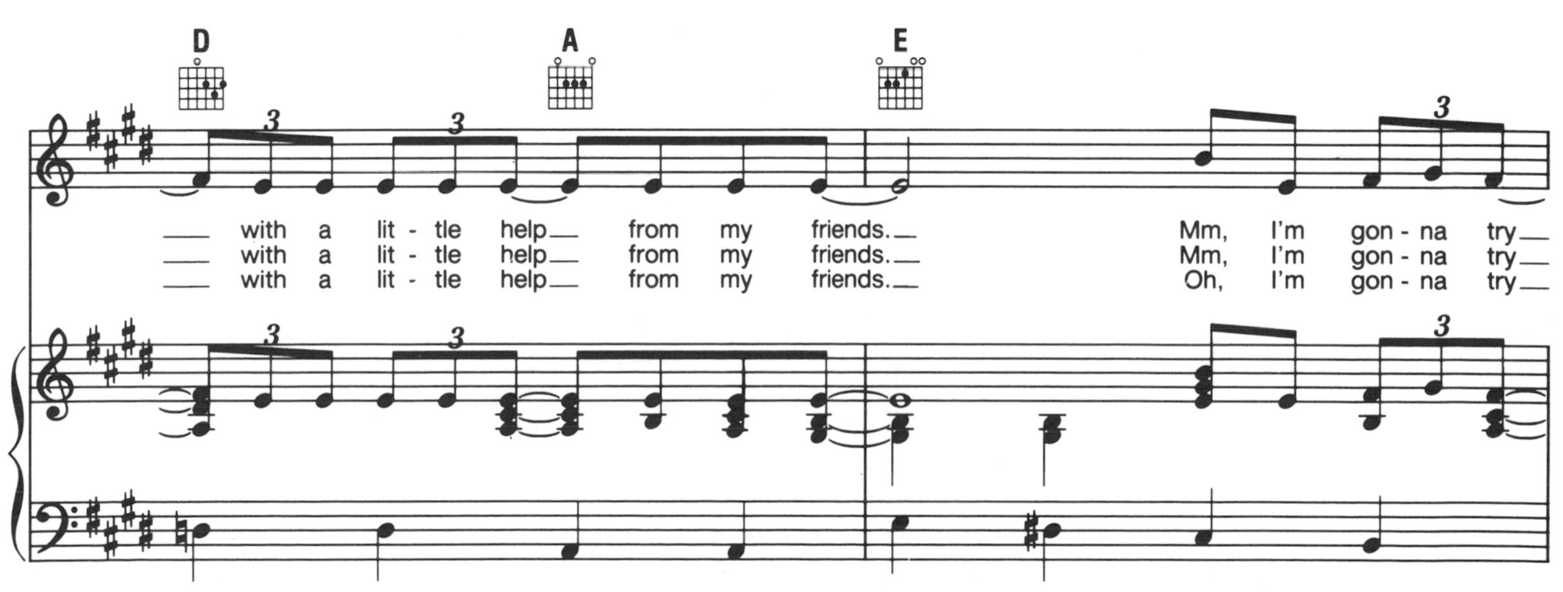
D
A
E
with a lit - tle help from my friends. Mm, I'm gon - na try
with a lit - tle help from my friends. Mm, I'm gon - na try
with a lit - tle help from my friends. Oh, I'm gon - na try
3
3

A
1
E
B7
with a lit - tle help from my friends.
with a lit - tle help from my friends.
with a lit - tle help from my friends.
2,3.
E
C♯m
F♯7
(Do you need any - y - bod - y?) I
(Do you need any - y - bod - y?) I
E
D
A
C♯m
need some - bod - y to love. (Could it be an - y - bod -
just need some - one to love. (Could it be an - y - bod -
F♯7
E
D
To Coda
A
D.S. al Coda
(3rd ending)
- y?) I want some - bod - y to love.
- y?) I want some - bod - y to love.

CODA
A
D
A
Oh, I get by with a lit-tle help from my friends.
E
D
A
E
Mm, I'm gon-na try with a lit-tle help from my friends. Oh, I get high
A
E
D
with a lit-tle help from my friends. Yes, I get by with a lit-tle help from my friends,
A
C/G
Am6
E
with a lit-tle help from my friends.

WITHOUT US

Theme from the Paramount Television Series FAMILY TIES

Words and Music by JEFF BARRY
and TOM SCOTT

G9sus
G9
B♭m6/D♭
mil - lion more.
Oh, it's
like I start - ed breath - in' on the night
had it planned,
ooo, it's
like we share a se - cret we could nev -
F/C
A7sus
A7
we kissed,
and I can't re - mem - ber what I ev - er
- er tell,
'cause no one else but you and me could ev -
C/D
D7
Gmaj7
did be - fore.
er un - der - stand.
What would we do ba - by, with - out us?
Bm7
Cmaj9
G/A
A6
A7
What would we do ba - by, with - out us?
And there ain't
mf

Am7
Cm9
Bm7
2 fr
E9
no noth - in' we can't love each oth - er through.
What would we do
To Coda
1
A7sus
A7
Cmaj7
Bm7
Am7
C/D
G/D
ba - by, with - out us?
Sha la la la.
A/C#
A9/C#
B♭6/C
If it's
mf
sfz
dim.
2
Cmaj7
Bm7
Am7
C/D
G/D
Sha la la la.
mf

A/C#
A9/C#
Cmaj7
Bm7
2 fr
Am7
B7#5
Em7
A7
You've got my num - ber,
and I know you know it.
C/D
G
F#7#9
3 fr
B7#5
Em7
And I'm stick-in' with you till the end.
A7
Ooo, I'm in trou - ble.
If I ev - er lost you,

C/D
Am7
Bm7
2fr
Cmaj7
B7
Em7
spend my whole life
look-in' for you a - gain.
cresc.
A7
You've got my num - ber;
you've got my num - ber;
C/D
Gmaj7
F#7#9
3fr
B7
Em7
you've got my num - ber.
dim.
A7
mf

G/D
C#dim7
Cmaj7
Bm7
2 fr
Am7
C/D
D.S. al Coda
What would we do
cresc.
CODA
Cmaj7
Bm7
Am7
Bm7
Em7
Sha la la la.
A7
You've got my num - ber;
you've got my num - ber;
Repeat ad lib. and Fade
C/D
Am7
Bm7
C
Bm7
Em7
you've got my num - ber.
Sha la la la.

WON'T YOU BE MY NEIGHBOR?
(It's a Beautiful Day in This Neighborhood)
from MISTER ROGERS' NEIGHBORHOOD

Words and Music by
FRED ROGERS

A♭m7
D♭
Gm11
C7
F6/9
Cm7
D7
hood with you.___ So let's make the most of this beau-ti-ful day,
Gm9
B♭m7
F
Dm7
Gm7
since we're to-geth-er we might as well say; Would you be mine? Could you be mine?
C7
F
B♭
Am7
Gm
Am7
D7
To Coda
Won't you be my neigh-bor? Won't you please, won't you please?
Gm7
C7
B♭
F
D.C. al Coda (with repeat)
Please won't you be my neigh-bor?___
CODA
Gm7
C7
B♭
F
Please won't you be my neigh-bor?___

YAKETY SAX

featured in the Television Series THE BENNY HILL SHOW

Words and Music by JAMES RICH
and BOOTS RANDOLPH

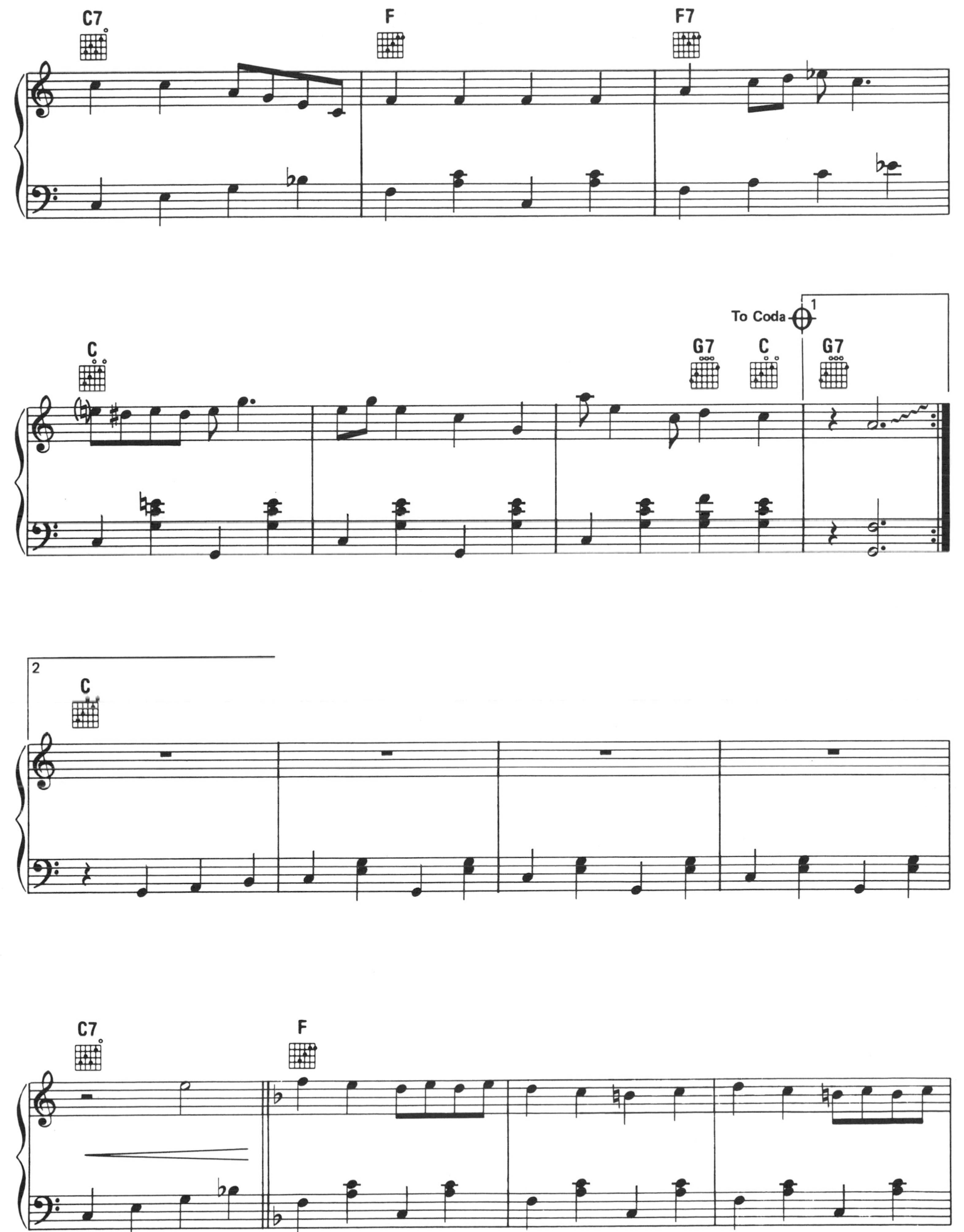
C7
F
F7
C
To Coda
1
G7
C
G7
2
C
C7
F

C7

F
F7
B♭

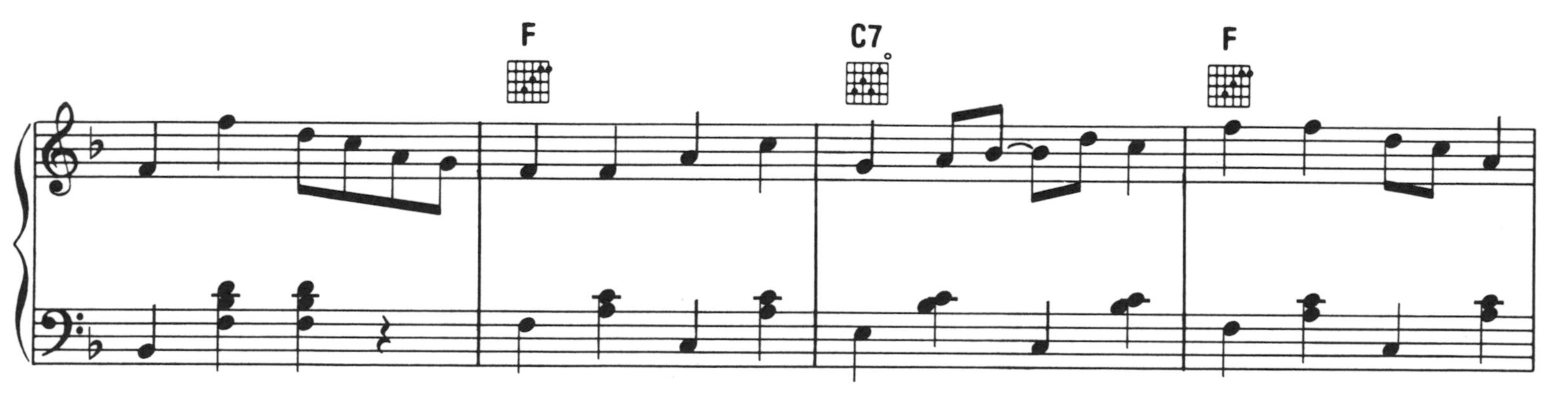
F
C7
F

mf

C7
f
F
F7
B♭7
F
C7
F
C7
F
D.C. al Coda
CODA
G7
C

THE ULTIMATE SERIES

This comprehensive series features jumbo collections of piano/vocal arrangements with guitar chords. Each volume features an outstanding selection of your favorite songs. Collect them all for the ultimate music library!

Blues
90 blues classics, including: Boom Boom • Born Under a Bad Sign • Gee Baby, Ain't I Good to You • I Can't Quit You Baby • Pride and Joy • (They Call It) Stormy Monday • Sweet Home Chicago • Why I Sing the Blues • You Shook Me • and more.
00310723 ....$19.95

Broadway Gold
100 show tunes: Beauty and the Beast • Do-Re-Mi • I Whistle a Happy Tune • The Lady Is a Tramp • Memory • My Funny Valentine • Oklahoma • Some Enchanted Evening • Summer Nights • Tomorrow • many more.
00361396 ....$21.95

Broadway Platinum
100 popular Broadway show tunes, featuring: Consider Yourself • Getting to Know You • Gigi • Do You Hear the People Sing • I'll Be Seeing You • My Favorite Things • People • She Loves Me • Try to Remember • Younger Than Springtime • many more.
00311496 ....$19.95

Children's Songbook
66 fun songs for kids: Alphabet Song • Be Our Guest • Bingo • The Brady Bunch • Do-Re-Mi • Hakuna Matata • It's a Small World • Kum Ba Yah • Sesame Street Theme • Tomorrow • Won't You Be My Neighbor? • and more.
00310690 ....$18.95

Christmas – Third Edition
Includes: Carol of the Bells • Deck the Hall • Frosty the Snow Man • Gesu Bambino • Good King Wenceslas • Jingle-Bell Rock • Joy to the World • Nuttin' for Christmas • O Holy Night • Rudolph the Red-Nosed Reindeer • Silent Night • What Child Is This? • and more.
00361399 ....$19.95

Country – Second Edition
90 of your favorite country hits: Boot Scootin' Boogie • Chattahoochie • Could I Have This Dance • Crazy • Down at the Twist And Shout • Hey, Good Lookin' • Lucille • When She Cries • and more.
00310036 ....$19.95

Gospel – 100 Songs of Devotion
Includes: El Shaddai • His Eye Is on the Sparrow • How Great Thou Art • Just a Closer Walk With Thee • Lead Me, Guide Me • (There'll Be) Peace in the Valley (For Me) • Precious Lord, Take My Hand • Wings of a Dove • more.
00241009 ....$19.95

Jazz Standards
Over 100 great jazz favorites: Ain't Misbehavin' • All of Me • Come Rain or Come Shine • Here's That Rainy Day • I'll Take Romance • Imagination • Li'l Darlin' • Manhattan • Moonglow • Moonlight in Vermont • A Night in Tunisia • The Party's Over • Solitude • Star Dust • and more.
00361407 ....$19.95

Latin Songs
80 hot Latin favorites, including: Amapola (Pretty Little Poppy) • Amor • Bésame Mucho (Kiss Me Much) • Blame It on the Bossa Nova • Feelings (¿Dime?) • Malagueña • Mambo No. 5 • Perfidia • Slightly out of Tune (Desafinado) • What a Diff'rence a Day Made • more.
00310689 ....$19.95

Love and Wedding Songbook
90 songs of devotion including: The Anniversary Waltz • Canon in D • Endless Love • Forever and Ever, Amen • Just the Way You Are • Love Me Tender • Sunrise, Sunset • Through the Years • Trumpet Voluntary • and more!
00361445 ....$19.95

Movie Music
73 favorites from the big screen, including: Can You Feel the Love Tonight • Chariots of Fire • Cruella De Vil • Driving Miss Daisy • Easter Parade • Forrest Gump • Moon River • That Thing You Do! • Viva Las Vegas • The Way We Were • When I Fall in Love • and more.
00310240 ....$18.95

For More Information, See Your Local Music Dealer, Or Write To:

7777 W. Bluemound Rd. P.O. Box 13819 Milwaukee, WI 53213

http://www.halleonard.com

Prices, contents, and availability subject to change without notice. Availability and pricing may vary outside the U.S.A.

Nostalgia Songs
100 great favorites from yesteryear, such as: Ain't We Got Fun? • Alexander's Ragtime Band • Casey Jones • Chicago • Danny Boy • Second Hand Rose • Swanee • Toot, Toot, Tootsie! • 'Way Down Yonder in New Orleans • The Yellow Rose of Texas • You Made Me Love You • and more!
00310730 ....$17.95

Rock 'N' Roll
100 classics, including: All Shook Up • Bye Bye Love • Duke of Earl • Gloria • Hello Mary Lou • It's My Party • Johnny B. Goode • The Loco-Motion • Lollipop • Surfin' U.S.A. • The Twist • Wooly Bully • Yakety Yak • and more.
00361411 ....$21.95

Singalong!
100 of the best-loved popular songs ever: Beer Barrel Polka • Crying in the Chapel • Edelweiss • Feelings • Five Foot Two, Eyes of Blue • For Me and My Gal • Indiana • It's a Small World • Que Sera, Sera • This Land Is Your Land • When Irish Eyes Are Smiling • and more.
00361418 ....$18.95

Standard Ballads
91 mellow masterpieces, including: Angel Eyes • Body and Soul • Darn That Dream • Day By Day • Easy to Love • Isn't It Romantic? • Misty • Mona Lisa • Moon River • My Funny Valentine • Smoke Gets in Your Eyes • When I Fall in Love • and more.
00310246 ....$19.95

Swing Standards
93 songs to get you swinging, including: Bandstand Boogie • Boogie Woogie Bugle Boy • Heart and Soul • How High the Moon • In the Mood • Moonglow • Satin Doll • Sentimental Journey • Witchcraft • and more.
00310245 ....$19.95

TV Themes
More than 90 themes from your favorite TV shows, including: The Addams Family Theme • Cleveland Rocks • Theme from Frasier • Happy Days • Love Boat Theme • Hey, Hey We're the Monkees • Nadia's Theme • Sesame Street Theme • Theme from Star Trek® • and more.
00310841 ....$19.95

0402

Contemporary Classics

Your favorite songs for piano, voice and guitar.

The Definitive Rock 'n' Roll Collection

A classic collection of the best songs from the early rock 'n' roll years – 1955-1966. 97 songs, including: Barbara Ann • Chantilly Lace • Dream Lover • Duke of Earl • Earth Angel • Great Balls of Fire • Louie, Louie • Rock Around the Clock • Ruby Baby • Runaway • (Seven Little Girls) Sitting in the Back Seat • Stay • Surfin' U.S.A. • Wild Thing • Woolly Bully • and more.

00490195 ....$29.95

The Big Book of Rock

78 of rock's biggest hits, including: Addicted to Love • American Pie • Born to Be Wild • Cold As Ice • Dust in the Wind • Free Bird • Goodbye Yellow Brick Road • Groovin' • Hey Jude • I Love Rock 'N' Roll • Lay Down Sally • Layla • Livin' on a Prayer • Louie Louie • Maggie May • Me and Bobby McGee • Monday, Monday • Owner of a Lonely Heart • Shout • Walk This Way • We Didn't Start the Fire • You Really Got Me • and more.

00311566..........$19.95

Big Book of Movie Music

Features 73 classic songs from 72 movies: Beauty and the Beast • Change the World • Eye of the Tiger • I Finally Found Someone • The John Dunbar Theme • Somewhere in Time • Stayin' Alive • Take My Breath Away • Unchained Melody • The Way You Look Tonight • You've Got a Friend in Me • Zorro's Theme • more.

00311582 ....$19.95

The Best Rock Songs Ever

70 of the best rock songs from yesterday and today, including: All Day and All of the Night • All Shook Up • Blue Suede Shoes • Born to Be Wild • Boys Are Back in Town • Every Breath You Take • Faith • Free Bird • Hey Jude • I Still Haven't Found What I'm Looking For • Livin' on a Prayer • Lola • Louie Louie • Maggie May • Money • (She's) Some Kind of Wonderful • Takin' Care of Business • Walk This Way • We Didn't Start the Fire • We Got the Beat • Wild Thing • more!

00490424..........$18.95

Contemporary Vocal Groups

This exciting new collection includes 35 huge hits by 18 of today's best vocal groups, including 98 Degrees, TLC, Destiny's Child, Savage Garden, Boyz II Men, Dixie Chicks, 'N Sync, and more! Songs include: Bills, Bills, Bills • Bug a Boo • Diggin' on You • The Hardest Thing • I'll Make Love to You • In the Still of the Nite (I'll Remember) • Ready to Run • Tearin' Up My Heart • Truly, Madly, Deeply • Waterfalls • Wide Open Spaces • and more.

00310605 ....$14.95

Motown Anthology

This songbook commemorates Motown's 40th Anniversary with 68 songs, background information on this famous record label, and lots of photos. Songs include: ABC • Baby Love • Ben • Dancing in the Street • Easy • For Once in My Life • My Girl • Shop Around • The Tracks of My Tears • War • What's Going On • You Can't Hurry Love • and many more.

00310367 ....$19.95

Best Contemporary Ballads

Includes 35 favorites: And So It Goes • Angel • Beautiful in My Eyes • Don't Know Much • Fields of Gold • Hero • I Will Remember You • Iris • My Heart Will Go On • Tears in Heaven • Valentine • You Were Meant for Me • You'll Be in My Heart • and more.

00310583 ....$16.95

Contemporary Hits

Contains 35 favorites by artists such as Sarah McLachlan, Whitney Houston, 'N Sync, Mariah Carey, Christina Aguilera, Celine Dion, and other top stars. Songs include: Adia • Building a Mystery • The Hardest Thing • I Believe in You and Me • I Drive Myself Crazy • I'll Be • Kiss Me • My Father's Eyes • Reflection • Smooth • Torn • and more!

00310589..........$16.95

Jock Rock Hits

32 stadium-shaking favorites, including: Another One Bites the Dust • The Boys Are Back In Town • Freeze-Frame • Gonna Make You Sweat (Everybody Dance Now) • I Got You (I Feel Good) • Na Na Hey Hey Kiss Him Goodbye • Rock & Roll – Part II (The Hey Song) • Shout • Tequila • We Are the Champions • We Will Rock You • Whoomp! (There It Is) • Wild Thing • and more.

00310105..........$14.95

Rock Ballads

31 sentimental favorites, including: All for Love • Bed of Roses • Dust in the Wind • Everybody Hurts • Right Here Waiting • Tears in Heaven • and more.

00311673..........$14.95

FOR MORE INFORMATION, SEE YOUR LOCAL MUSIC DEALER,
OR WRITE TO:

7777 W. BLUEMOUND RD. P.O. BOX 13819 MILWAUKEE, WI 53213

Visit Hal Leonard Online at www.halleonard.com

Prices, contents & availability subject to change without notice.

Big Books of Music

Our "Big Books" feature big selections of popular titles under one cover, perfect for performing musicians, music aficionados or the serious hobbyist. All books are arranged for piano, voice, and guitar, and feature stay-open binding, so the books lie flat without breaking the spine.

BIG BOOK OF BALLADS
63 songs.
00310485 ....$19.95

BIG BOOK OF BIG BAND HITS
84 songs.
00310701 ....$19.95

BIG BOOK OF BROADWAY
70 songs.
00311658 ....$19.95

BIG BOOK OF CHILDREN'S SONGS
55 songs.
00359261 ....$14.95

GREAT BIG BOOK OF CHILDREN'S SONGS
76 songs.
00310002 ....$14.95

MIGHTY BIG BOOK OF CHILDREN'S SONGS
65 songs.
00310467 ....$14.95

REALLY BIG BOOK OF CHILDREN'S SONGS
63 songs.
00310372 ....$15.95

BIG BOOK OF CHILDREN'S MOVIE SONGS
66 songs.
00310731 ....$17.95

BIG BOOK OF CHRISTMAS SONGS
126 songs.
00311520 ....$19.95

BIG BOOK OF CLASSIC ROCK
77 songs.
00310801 ....$19.95

REALLY BIG BOOK OF CHILDREN'S SONGS
63 songs.
00310372 ....$15.95

BIG BOOK OF CLASSICAL MUSIC
100 songs.
00310508 ....$19.95

BIG BOOK OF CONTEMPORARY CHRISTIAN FAVORITES
50 songs.
00310021 ....$19.95

BIG BOOK OF COUNTRY MUSIC
64 songs.
00310188 ....$19.95

BIG BOOK OF EARLY ROCK N' ROLL
99 songs.
00310398 ....$19.95

BIG BOOK OF GOLDEN OLDIES
73 songs.
00310756 ....$19.95

BIG BOOK OF GOSPEL SONGS
100 songs.
00310604 ....$19.95

BIG BOOK OF HYMNS
125 hymns.
00310510 ....$17.95

BIG BOOK OF JAZZ
75 songs.
00311557 ....$19.95

BIG BOOK OF LATIN AMERICAN SONGS
89 songs.
00311562 ....$19.95

BIG BOOK OF LOVE SONGS
80 songs.
00310784 ....$19.95

BIG BOOK OF MOVIE MUSIC
72 songs.
00311582 ....$19.95

BIG BOOK OF NOSTALGIA
158 songs.
00310004 ....$19.95

BIG BOOK OF RHYTHM & BLUES
67 songs.
00310169 ....$19.95

BIG BOOK OF ROCK
78 songs.
00311566 ....$19.95

BIG BOOK OF SOUL SONGS
71 songs.
00310771 ....$19.95

BIG BOOK OF STANDARDS
86 songs.
00311667 ....$19.95

BIG BOOK OF SWING
84 songs.
00310359 ....$19.95

BIG BOOK OF TORCH SONGS
75 songs.
00310561 ....$19.95

BIG BOOK OF TV THEME SONGS
78 songs.
00310504 ....$19.95

BIG BOOK OF WEDDING MUSIC
78 songs.
00311567 ....$19.95

For More Information, See Your Local Music Dealer, Or Write To:

HAL•LEONARD® CORPORATION

7777 W. Bluemound Rd. P.O. Box 13819 Milwaukee, WI 53213

Prices, contents, and availability subject to change without notice.

Visit **www.halleonard.com** for our entire catalog and to view our complete songlists.